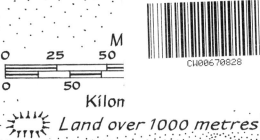
M
O   25   50
O   50
Kilon

☼ Land over 1000 metres

– K h a l í

D H O F A R

Al-Gheidha •

Tarím
Qabr Hud
Aynat
W. Hadhramaut   Seiyun
Shibam   Al-Ghurfa
Al-Qaṭn
Horeidha
Hajarayn
H A D H R A M A U T   M A H R A
W. Masilah
Qishn
Seihut
Khoreiba
W. Doan
Gheil Ba Wazir
Mola Matar
Harshyat
Baqrain
W. Hajr   Shihr
Mayfa'a   Bir Ali   Mukalla
Cana
Balhaf

A R A B I A N   S E A

D E N
Km
O   100
Qallansiyya   Hadibu   Suq   54°
SOCOTRA   Eriosh   Haggeher Mts.
Abd al-Kuri
Samhah   Darsa
54°   12°

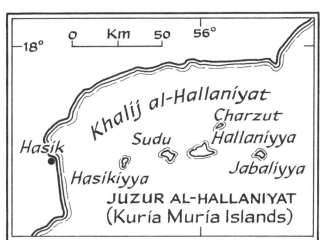

Km
18°   O   50   56°
Khalij al-Hallaniyat
Charzut
Sudu   Hallaniyya
Hasik
Hasikiyya   Jabaliyya
JUZUR AL-HALLANIYAT
(Kuria Muria Islands)

YEMEN

ENGRAVED

Yemen Engraved

published by

Stacey International
128 Kensington Church Street
London W8 4BH
Tel: 020 7221 7166 Fax: 020 7792 9288
E-mail: enquiries@stacey-international.co.uk
Website: www.stacey-international.co.uk

© Stacey International 2006

ISBN: 1900988 704

CIP Data: A catalogue record for this book is
available from the British Library

Design: Kitty Carruthers
Printing & Binding: SNP Leefung, China

Transliteration: words and place names have been anglicized
wherever possible, for example Mocha and Seihut.

The publishers wish to thank those who helped to bring this work into being:

www.utcyemen.com

Universal Group

مجلس الترويج السياحي
Tourism Promotion Board

YEMEN
ENGRAVED

Illustrations by
foreign travellers
1680-1903

Leila Ingrams

To the men, women and children of Yemen
and with deep gratitude to my parents,
who introduced me to them and the country.

CONTENTS

ACKNOWLEDGEMENTS

I would like to extend my special thanks to the friends who have assisted me with this work.

Mr Alwan Al Shaibani, Chairman, Universal Group and Marco Livadiotti, General Manager, Universal Touring Company have been of particular help. The idea of gathering for the first time engravings by foreign travellers to Ethiopia was that of Professor Richard Pankhurst – those engravings formed *Ethiopia Engraved*; *Yemen Engraved* is a companion volume. I am greatly indebted to Richard for reading through the entire work, for writing the preface, and for the loan of books from his library; and to Professor Rex Smith who also read through the entire work and to Sultan Ghalib Al-Qu'aiti for reading the text. I am most grateful to all three for generously giving me their kind scholarly advice, which has been invaluable. Naturally, they are not responsible for my mistakes.

It is a great privilege that Professor Saleh Ali Bassurah has written the Foreword to this book. Our families' friendship goes back many years to when my parents received the most generous and memorable hospitality from the Basurrah family in the ancient valley of Do'an and were invited to taste, for the first time, the famous Do'ani honey – 'lovely round golden combs too beautiful to cut.'

My special thanks are also due to Mustafa Rajamanar for all his assistance; Ted Hatch at the Royal Geographical Society for his painstaking work on the map, drawn to illustrate *Yemen Engraved*; to Margaret Stapley and Edward Walters; to the staff of: the British Library, *The Illustrated London News*, the Linnean Society, the National Arts Library of Great Britain, the Natural History Museum and Library, the Royal Asiatic Society, the Royal Geographical Society and to Denis Gérard for scanning to disc the engravings from books in Professor Pankhurst's library.

I want to add my warmest thanks to Tom Stacey and Max Scott for instigating the publication of this work, Kitty Carruthers for her skilful work on design and Caroline Williams for all her help.

Leila Ingrams
January 2006

FOREWORD

For thousands of years Yemen has drawn travellers from around the world to its shores for many reasons but perhaps most importantly because of its strategic geographical location and the wealth of its natural resources: particularly frankincense and myrrh. The country became well known to the outside world through word of mouth of early travellers and later through their writings. Yemen is quoted in the Torah and the Holy Qu'ran, ancient inscriptions and stories, one of the most famous being the story of the Queen of Sheba. Yemeni cities and places are considered to be historic museums namely the old city of Sana'a. Shibam of Hadhramaut, Wadi Do'an and its villages, Tarim, Sa'ada, Zabid and many more. Many of the foreigners who visited Yemen had a particular goal; political, geographical, scientific, religious and tourism and many recorded what they had observed.

I have the honour to write this Foreword to Yemen Engraved by Leila Ingrams. It is an important document on the heritage of Yemen as portrayed by foreign travellers from 1496 to the turn of the 20th century, although the copies of early illustrations contained herein, date from 1680 because the originals have deteriorated. We, in Yemen, owe our sincere gratitude and deep appreciation to these travellers and artists for bringing Yemen and its history to the outside world. We render to Leila our heartfelt congratulations for successfully gathering, for the first time, this volume of knowledge of our country, Yemen. In this work, she has confirmed and deepened her love for Yemen and its people which started in her very early childhood and when her parents gave her the Arab Bedouin name of Leila.

Finally, I wish Leila Ingrams health, happiness, prosperity and success in all her work and an everlasting love of Yemen.

Professor Saleh Ali Bassurah
Minister for Higher Education and Scientific Research
Former Rector, University of Sana'a

Sana'a
January 2006

'*Wanderer if you come to the land of the Sabaeans, do not fear the sun;
for the shade of the trees will follow you wherever you go.*'

Traditional

PREFACE

Yemen is a land of great antiquity. The country is likewise a place of immense natural beauty, with tall mountains sculptured with hand-carved terraces and deep ravines with waterfalls tumbling over rocks, trees and flowers. Parched plateaux contrast with shimmering lush vegetation, the abode, in the past, of abundant wild-life.

Yemen is also the location of many unique buildings – the multi-storeyed 'skyscrapers' of ancient times, and unforgettably beautiful mosques and minarets. It is the site of one of the world's great civilisations, whose cultural importance has been recognised by UNESCO.

The country over the centuries attracted the attention of numerous foreign travellers. Some made Yemen their main destination, while others tarried there when bound for other lands: Ethiopia and the Horn of Africa to the west, as well as British India and countries further East.

Visiting travellers included several distinguished artists, most notably from Britain, Denmark, France, Germany, Italy and Sweden. Their sketches and drawings, now largely forgotten, formed the basis of the engravings reproduced in this volume. Such works capture and preserve rare glimpses of the country.

Many of the finest and most revealing engravings of old-time Yemen, taken on the whole from books, have here for the first time been most skilfully gathered into one volume. Its author, Leila Ingrams, has long been interested in Yemen. Her mother and father, who in the 1930s and 1940s were the first 'foreign travellers' from the West to make Hadhramaut their home, are legends inside and outside the country. She co-edited, with her mother, a vast sixteen-volume reference work *Records of Yemen 1798 to 1960*. Leila also co-authored a companion volume with me, *Ethiopia Engraved*, which sought to document Ethiopia's no less colourful past.

Yemen Engraved is a labour of love. In itself it is a work of art, and a valuable historical document: valuable for the light it throws on the country's past: economic, social, cultural, religious and political, as well as on the artistic interests and values of the European travellers whose pictorial images Leila has painstakingly saved from oblivion.

The book opens with a panoramic overview of the Yemeni geographical setting, with its mountains and abysses, and of the country's famed buildings, architectural traditions, and hard-working population. We see Yemeni men and women vividly portrayed in their traditional dress, and gain an insight into their agricultural and pastoral life.

The volume then proceeds to an examination of the famous cities of Sana'a and Aden; the grandeur of the Hadhramaut valley with its astonishing architecture; the Red Sea plain of the Tihamah with its fabled port of Mocha and its links with Africa; and of Yemen's beautiful but vulnerable off-shore islands. The region's notable early past is also represented: intriguing old graffiti, and exciting relief carvings of figures found in the renowned Marib region; the splendid 'Yemeni' temple of Yeha across the sea in northern Ethiopia; and ancient Yemeni inscriptions in monumental South Arabian script. We see Yemen's unique position between the Red Sea, Gulf of Aden and Arabian Sea. These waters were well known to Yemeni navigators, who at first hugged the coast, but later ventured much further in quest of trade with the outside world. The penultimate section is devoted to the country's flora and fauna. Finally there are portraits of the artists of yesteryear who made this important volume possible. No less fascinating are the drawings of the camp of the German scientific mission in Socotra in 1881; and of the guest house of the Sultan of Lahej, where British scientists stayed before their visit to Socotra.

Yemen Engraved should prove an invaluable research tool for everyone interested in Yemeni history and culture, as well as an appealing book for foreign visitors, journalists and film-makers, who may find this study an aid and inspiration for their work.

Richard Pankhurst
Professor of Ethiopian Studies
Institute of Ethiopian Studies
Addis Ababa

INTRODUCTION

'Wisdom belongs to al-Yemen; the foundation
of all things is here; all things have their origin in al-Yemen'

Traditional

Al-Yemen ~ the Fortunate ~ is the ancient name given by the Arabs to the south and south-western corner of Jezirat al-Arab, the Island or Peninsula of Arabia. Known as the 'Garden of Arabia', it was a fertile and prosperous land. To the Romans it was Arabia Felix, 'Arabia the Blessed'. *The Periplus of the Erythraean Sea*, a detailed Graeco-Egyptian seafarer's manual written anonymously in the first century AD gives to what is now the modern port of Aden, the name *Eudaemon Arabia*, and this became the name of the entire district. With the rise of Islam, Arab geographers regarded al-Yemen more in its other meaning of the 'Right Side' or the 'Right Hand', as it lay to the right of the Holy Land of Hejaz.

Much of Yemen's ancient history survives in legends, proverbs and poems handed down by word of mouth, and in inscriptions found on many ancient sites and along old caravan routes. Frontiers then existed only through the power of any particular state to hold a territory, and the tribal states that spread over the country were constantly changing. From around 1,000 BC until the early centuries AD there were four dominant kingdoms: Ma'in, Saba', Qataban, and Hadhramaut. These kingdoms rose to prominence at successive or overlapping periods and their power and influence are integral to the country's history. Even into the twentieth and twenty-first centuries their names have survived. Echoes of the Minaean Kingdom were heard in the deliberations of the Grand Council of the Ma'in tribe, the Sabaeans in the Beni Saba', Qataban in Ahl Quteib, Hadhramaut in Hadhramaut. Awsan is also thought to have been a separate kingdom, although the latest academic opinion disputes this. Many tribes all over Yemen claim descent from the later Himyarites. The influence of Himyar in the centuries just prior to Islam was so strong that today 'Himyaritic' or 'Himyarite' is the name often given to all South Arabian antiquities and inscriptions of different states and periods. The Imams of Yemen asserted Himyarite descent, which they symbolised by marking their dispatches with red ochre; the word for red (*ahmar*), and Himyar, have the same root in Arabic.

Frankincense and myrrh, both valuable commodities, were produced in the area. The perfumed resins constituted an indispensable part of religious rites in ancient Rome, Greece, Mesapotamia, Arabia and Egypt. To the Pharaohs incense was so highly prized that they themselves offered it to their gods to please them, and they had been sending expeditions to the Land of Punt long before that of Queen Hatshepsut in about 1500 BC, the events of which are splendidly illustrated in a series of reliefs on the walls of her temple at Deir al-Bahri, near Thebes. Punt is an area which may never have been precisely defined. Opinions are divided as to the exact location of Punt: Upper Egypt, Somalia, Eritrea, East Sudan, Ethiopia, and South Arabia have all been considered possible, as they were the regions where frankincense and myrrh grew, although in recent times some scholars think that Punt could not have been in South Arabia. The name myrrh is derived from the Arabic *murr* meaning 'bitter' on account of its taste. In Yemen, frankincense and myrrh trees are found mostly in Hadhramaut, Mahra and Socotra.

11

These resins were important not only to the Egyptians but also to the Persians, Indians, Greeks and Romans. Herodotus, who was born in the Greek city of Halicarnassus, south-west Asia Minor in about 485 BC, and was known as the 'father of history', records the first of the expeditions of conquest to the incense lands, drawn as it were by the magnet of their reputed prosperity. In about 500 BC the Persian king Darius sent Scylax of Caryanda down the Indus on a thirty-month voyage which took him to Suez via Oman, the South Arabian coast and the Red Sea. Doubt has been cast upon this expedition, but whether it took place or not it would seem that the Persian king had some success as the Arabians sent him a yearly gift of one thousand talents weight of frankincense. Plutarch, biographer and philosopher, recounted in his *Life* of Alexander III, 'the Great', how Alexander, when a boy, heaped frankincense on the altars in such lavish fashion that his tutor Leonidas told him that he might 'worship the gods in that manner when he had conquered the frankincense-growing races.' Taking his tutor's words to heart, Alexander sent an expedition to circumnavigate Arabia. His admiral, Hieron, sailed down the eastern Gulf to Ras Musandam, whilst Admiral Anaxicrates sailed down the Red Sea through the Bab al-Mandab Strait to the south coast of Arabia. Alexander's sudden death of a fever in Babylon in 323 BC brought his ideas of conquest to an end.

In 24 BC Emperor Augustus appointed his Prefect of Egypt, Marcus Aelius Gallus, to lead the Tenth Legion into south-west Arabia, an expedition described in Strabo of Pontus' *Geography* from a report received by someone who had accompanied the ill-fated expedition. According to Strabo, it was doomed from the outset, as its guide was a Nabataean, whose people controlled much of the northern incense route, and thrived on the profits of the trade. The guide feared, not without reason, that the Romans were not coming as traders but had political and military objectives. Consequently the legion was misguided through the arid region and the climate and conditions took their toll. Disease, hunger and the difficult terrain forced Aelius Gallus to abandon the expedition and return to Egypt.

Greek and Roman scholars who wrote of the incense lands must have gleaned much of their information from such expeditions and from traders travelling overland with caravans, or coasting along the shores. These men would have been able to give the names of places on main caravan routes, and provided valuable information that was used by the geographer, Ptolemy, in his map of the second century AD.

The majority of the population was not concerned with the incense trade but with agriculture and irrigation, which were vital for their economic prosperity. The Sabaeans had particular skills in building highly organised irrigation schemes, the most famous being the dam at Marib, the Sabaean capital. Strabo also noted the incense lands as being 'watered by summer rains and are sowed twice, like India; and the rivers there are used up in supplying plains and lakes. The country is in general fertile and abounds in particular with places for making honey … it has an abundance of domesticated animals … [and] all kinds of birds.'

On the south coast a few miles away from the small harbour of Bir Ali lie the ruins of the ancient port of Cana, where many of the incense caravans began their journey to the Mediterranean from around the first century AD. Cargoes of incense were carried on inflated rafts made of skins or in ships from Dhofar, Socotra and other coastal places to Cana. Travellers by sea or land could identify Cana by a conspicuous landmark against the shining white sand of the shore: a big volcanic rock known as *Husn al-Ghorab*, 'Fortress of the Crows'. Today, its solitary flattened crater is a prominent feature from the air. One route north was through the great fertile Wadi Mayfa'a, which the caravans followed until they reached the fortress town of Naqab al-Hajr, pre-Islamic Mayfa'at, surrounded by a massive stone wall. On his arrival at the ruins in 1835, Lieutenant J. R. Wellsted, a surveyor on board the East India Company ship, *Palinurus*, wrote: 'a rapid glance soon convinced me, that their examination would more than compensate for any fatigue or privations we had undergone on our road to them.' He continued: 'But independent of these ancient monuments in themselves ~ far more than enough to repay the adventurer ~ the conditions, character, and pursuits of the inhabitants, the productions, resources, and nature of the country, severally furnish subjects of peculiar interest, and would, there can be no doubt, amply repay the curiosity of the first European who should visit them.' Leaving Naqab al-Hajr, the incense caravans carried on through Wadi Jirdan which like Mayfa'a was another well irrigated and populated valley and finally across sandy stretches to Shabwah.

A more arduous caravan route from Cana to Shabwah ran due north through a pass in the mountains to Wadi Hajr. Here caravans were confronted by the enormous stone wall of Qalat, known locally as Qalat al-Mabna, which formed a frontier between the kingdoms of the coast and the interior. No frontier can have been better protected than Qalat al-Mabna, for it stretched over two hundred yards across every gully obstructing any possible way, and the caravans were forced to pass through a passage seven feet wide and seventeen feet long, flanked by a bastion on each side. An inscription in this passage was copied by Baron Adolphe von Wrede, a Bavarian solider who had served with the Greek army and was the first European to visit the interior of Hadhramaut, although he did not reach the main trunk of Wadi Hadhramaut. He landed in Mukalla in 1843. When the cameleers had guided their caravans through this passage, they clambered out of Wadi Hajr onto the uplands. The route then wended its way up and down mountain passes to Shabwah.

Shabwah, known to the Classical writers as Sabata or Sabota, may have been occupied as early as the mid-second millennium BC. Between the fifth century BC and fifth century AD it developed and became the capital of Hadhramaut. Inscriptions recording coronations and other ceremonies connected with the kings of Hadhramaut are to be found at al-Uqla, some ten miles from Shabwah. Pliny wrote of the Atramites whose capital city Sabota had within

Opposite: **'Bedouin of the opposite coast. The figure is believed to have been taken from a Christian church wherein were represented the characters of several tribes constituting the Ethiopian government of Aksum.'** *Bird*

Right: **This is a beautiful example of a certain style of South Arabian dedication. The bust has a twisted cord around the base and an inscription below. The dedicant is shown in a characteristic pose, with a raised right hand, and in the left hand holds a bird. The figure wears a round-necked tunic with short sleeves decorated at the edges and two decorated strips down the front. The plaited hair hangs over each shoulder.** *Bird*

13

its walls sixty temples; the marble used to build them was said to have come from Kilwa on the East African coast. Harry St. John Philby, (known as Jack or Sheikh Abdullah), and called by some the twentieth century's 'Greatest of Arabian Explorers', cast doubt on the existence of so many temples. Pliny's account, he said, was 'grossly inaccurate': there could never have been sixty temples, or even six, within the walls. He suggested that Pliny might have been referring to the whole district between the Yemen highlands and Shabwah. The incense traders, however, did build a great road known as Tariq 'Adiyya, or the Adite Way, paved with well-shaped stones and called after the legendary 'Ad, a man of athletic form and gigantic build, ancestor of the inhabitants of the incense lands who were known as the children of 'Ad.

The royal seat of Qataban, Timna, is thought to have been an important halting place for caravans when they left Shabwah. It lies at the mouth of Wadi Bayhan on a mound called Hajr Kohlan. Timna's rulers, like those of Saba', were termed *mukarribs*, priest-kings or federators, but were later replaced by 'kings of Saba". Not far from the ruins of Timna is the town of Bayhan, once famed for its horses. Two strains were particularly popular: *kubeishi* and *mu'ali*, considered superior to the horses of the high plateaux. The Portuguese tried cornering the important trade in horses to India but were opposed by the outstanding Hadhrami chieftain, Badr Bu Tuweirak bin Abdullah, when they attempted to interfere with his ports.

The ruins of Marib testify to the greatness of the Sabaeans, who Strabo described as a very large tribe with 'a vast equipment of both gold and silver articles such as couches, tripods and bowls, together with drinking vessels and very costly homes.' Pliny also remarked upon the wealth of the Sabaeans, 'which standeth upon their woods and trees, that bring forth the gummes of frankincense and myrrh, also in mines of Gold'. Legend relates

Stela in Aksum, northern Ethiopia, with Greek inscription *circa* **fourth century** AD. *Salt 411.*

that the Queen of Sheba ruled from Marib. Remains of a large temple, now known as 'Mahram Bilqis' ~ 'the Sanctuary of Bilqis' (the Yemeni name for the Queen of Sheba), stand near Marib. The Sabaeans had their first capital at Sirwah, where it is believed the Queen is buried. In the nineteenth century T. J. Arnaud, a French pharmacist, and Joseph Halévy on a mission for the Académie des Inscriptions of Paris were able to visit Marib briefly and the Austrian traveller, Eduard Glaser, spent a month there. They copied an enormous number of inscriptions but for a long time after the Imams became suspicious about the intentions of foreigners and forbade them to enter Marib. The bursting of the great dam at Marib early in the Christian era is mentioned in the Qur'an.

Yemen was part of the Kingdom of Aksum, which was established before the birth of Christ and at its height was the most powerful state between the Persian and the Roman Empires. Its capital was Aksum, situated in northern Ethiopia. Archaeological research at Marib has recently identified a number of inscriptions referring to the presence of Aksumites in the area, whose rulers are named *nagasi* of Habashat (King of Abyssinia). Notable Sabaean sites exist in Ethiopia and the temple of Yeha, north-east of Adwa, is one of the finest examples. Much of the building is still extant. Made with great precision and skill, its large blocks of limestone are held together without cement. Merchants of Yemen traded with the Aksumites whose principal port was Adulis, or Adulé, in the Bay of Zulla. During his journeys in Ethiopia in the early 1800s, Henry Salt, the British envoy and an excellent draftsman, drew magnificent views of the imposing stelae at Aksum. One of his illustrations shows a Greek text, one of the three on the stela, the other two being Sabaean and Ge'ez, which do not appear in his book *A Voyage to Abyssinia*. The links between Yemen and Ethiopia are apparent in the opening sentence of the inscription: '[We]

Translation of the Axum Inscription
adapted from Salt 411-412

[We] Aeizanas King of the Axomites and of the Homerites,
and of Raeidan, and of the Ethiopians and of the Sabeans [Sabaeans], and of Zeyla,
and of Tiamo and the Bója, and of the Taguie, king of kings, son of God,
the invincible Mars — having rebelled, on an occasion, the nation of the Bója.
We sent our brothers, Saiazana and Adephas to make war upon them,
and upon their surrender, [our brothers] after subduing them,
brought them to us, with their families; of their oxen,
and of their sheep, and their beasts bearing burthens;
nourishing them with the flesh of oxen, and giving them a supply of bread,
and affording them to drink beer, and wine, and water in abundance.
Who [the prisoners] were in number six chiefs, with their
multitude in number making them bread every day,
of wheaten cakes, and giving them wine for a month,
until the time that they brought them to us; whom, therefore,
supplying with all things fit, and clothing, we compelled to change their abode,
and sent them to a certain place of our country called M———a,
and we ordered them again to be supplied with bread,
furnishing to their six chiefs oxen.
In grateful acknowledgement to him who begat me,
the invincible Mars, I have dedicated to him
a golden statue, and one of silver, and three of brass, for good.

The Sabaean temple of Yeha, north-east of Adwa in Ethiopia. A huge temple 50 feet high, built with great skill and erected from large, perfectly shaped blocks of limestone held together without mortar. *Bent(2)136*

Above: Naqab al-Hajr, the walled fortress city known as Mayfa'at in the *Periplus.* 'The hill upon which [the ruins] are situated, stands out in the centre of the valley [of Mayfa'a, Hadhramaut], and divides a stream which passes, during floods, on either side of it. It is nearly 800 yards in length, and about 350 yards at its greatest breadth ... The ruins of Nakab al-Hajar, considered by themselves, present nothing therefore than a mass of ruins surrounded by a wall; but the magnitude of the stones with which this is built, the unity of conception and execution, exhibited in the style and mode of placing them together – with its towers, and its great extent, would stamp it as a work of considerable labour in any other part of the world ... The inscription which it has been our good fortune to discover, will, there is every reason to believe, create considerable interest among the learned.' *Wellsted(1)I.426*

Aeizanas King of the Axomites and of the Homerites, and of Raeidan [in Yemen], and of the Ethiopians and of the Sabeans [Sabaeans] ...'.

   Christianity came to Yemen at a very early date. Tradition has it that missionaries started work in apostolic times. In the fourth century, missionaries went to both sides of the Red Sea, and it has been claimed that Frumentius, apostle of Ethiopia, also visited south-west Arabia. More definite evidence exists that, in the reign of Constantius II, Theophilus Indus 'invested with the double character of ambassador and bishop', took charge of newly-

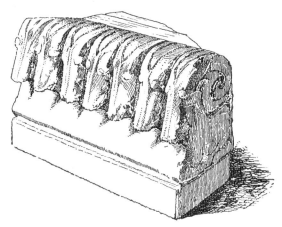

'Architectural fragment composed of alabaseroid [alabastrine] limestone, said to have come from Hadramaut' which represents 'seven chamois (or goats) lying in a row. The heads are coarsely formed, the eyes like knobs, and the bodies of the two animals which are outside are indicated in profile.'   *Bent(1)Appendix XIII*

formed churches in Ethiopia, south-west Arabia and Socotra. Theophilus founded a church in Aden and was permitted to build others in the city of Zafar, near Yarim.

Judaism also came to Yemen. Dhu Nuwas, the last Himyarite king reigned from AD 490-AD 525. He became a convert to Judaism and tried to force the religion on his subjects. During his reign, Dhu Nuwas plundered the predominantly Christian settlement of Najran, in what is now southern Saudi Arabia, and gave the people the choice between Judaism and death. When they chose death, large pits were dug and filled with burning fuel. About 20,000 people, including those who embraced a monastic life, refused to renounce Christianity, and were cast into the flames and killed by the sword. Amongst the victims was the head of the town, and Al-Masudi records in his *Meadows of Gold and Mines of Gems,* the heroism of a certain woman of Najran with her baby son of seven months. After this massacre, Dhu Nuwas was given the epithet of 'the Lord of the burning pit' and the fidelity of the martyrs, or 'brethren of the pit' is cited in the Qur'an. It is understood that King Kaleb of Aksum sent his commander and viceroy Abraha to Yemen. He is described in some accounts as a member of Kaleb's family. The Christians led by Abraha successfully invaded Yemen in AD 525 and he became an independent ruler of Yemen.

In AD 622, the Prophet Mohammed called on Arabia to follow the new faith of Islam which had been revealed to him. Most regions submitted to him. In AD 628, at a time when the Persians were overlords of Yemen, the last Persian satrap of Yemen obeyed the call, became a Muslim, and was confirmed in his post. Dissension among the Christians favoured the spread of the new religion, and there were several important converts. Christians also obtained favourable terms from the Prophet. The Prophet knew of Yemen and its people because of the regular caravans travelling to and from Yemen involved largely with trade. With the coming of Islam, rule from Persia gradually declined, to be replaced by the rule of Umayyad Caliphs in Damascus.

In AD 740 Zayd, the founder of the Zaydi dynasty, was killed at Kufa in Iraq after rebelling against the Umayyad Caliph. The Zaydi Imams claimed authority to rule as descendants of the Prophet through his daughter Fatima, wife of Ali ibn Abi Talib. The first Zaydi Imam, al-Hadi Yahya, migrated from Iraq with his father in about AD 870 and, after a sojourn in Sind, reached Sa'da in the north of Yemen. Yahya took the title of 'Leader unto Truth', or al-Hadi, and proclaimed himself Imam *circa* AD 885. Mohammed Hasan al-Hamdani, the famous South Arabian scholar of the tenth century, described Sa'da as a prominent centre for iron mining and for tanning. It was one of the main stations on the pre-Islamic trade route which connected Sana'a with Mecca. During the centuries after Yahya, Sa'da served as the capital and became an important school for Zaydi learning.

Gradually the pattern of rivalry in Yemen became established. Shiites in the highlands paid nominal homage to the Fatimid Caliphs in Egypt. They took their name from the Prophet's daughter, Fatima, and sought to set up some authority over Yemen. Sunnis in the lowlands paid their homage to the Abbasid Caliphs in Baghdad, who had followed the Umayyads of Damascus in AD 750. Within this pattern there were disagreements and petty dynasties. After the death of Ali ibn Abi Talib, the Caliphs of both these dynasties had sent their governors to Yemen to keep it under control, but apart from a time in the ninth century, they were not successful. The failure of these Caliphs would lead to periods of Egyptian occupation and a continuing Egyptian connection.

During the Egyptian period, Sana'a was the headquarters of the Sulayhids, 1047-1088. During his reign, Ali bin Mohammed, the leader, built a number of palaces in Sana'a and appointed his governors in the provinces. Ali bin Mohammed was succeeded by his son, al-Mukarram Ahmad, whose wife, Arwa, was called by the twelfth century historian and poet, Najm al-din Umarah al-Hakami, 'the honourable lady the Queen Sayyidah, daughter of Ahmad'. He wrote that al-Mukarram Ahmad 'made over the superintendence of affairs to his wife … He, on his part, gave himself up to the pleasures of music and wine.' In Sana'a she said to al-Mukarram, 'My Lord, send notice to the people of Sana'a to assemble tomorrow and to come unto this plain.' On their assembling she told him to cast down his eyes upon the people and to look at what he could see. He did so, and nothing met his eyes but the lightning-flashes of drawn swords and of lance-blades. On going to Dhu Jiblah she asked al-Mukarram to assemble its people and those of the neighbourhood. They gathered together on the morning of the following day, whereupon she said: 'Look down, my Lord, and behold these people.' He did so, and his eyes fell upon men leading rams or carrying vessels filled with ghee or with honey. 'Life among these (industrious) people', she told al-Mukarram, 'is to be preferred'. Control over Yemen was maintained by the strength of character and wisdom of this remarkable woman for fifty years from her capital Jiblah, near Ibb. Sana'a was then left in the hands of governors. Queen Arwa died in 1138 and is buried in Jiblah in the mosque named after her.

'One day we two, [Mabel and Theodore Bent] went some distance in the direction of the mountains and came on a large upright rock with an inscription upon it, evidently late Himyaritic or Ethiopic, and copied as much of it as was distinguishable ... Not far off was the tidy little hamlet of Haida [near Qallansiyya on Socotra].' *Bent(1)Appendix IV*

In 1173 Saladin (Salah al-Din ibn Ayyub), having made himself Sultan of Egypt after overthrowing the Fatimid Caliphate, sent his brother Turanshah to conquer Yemen, which he succeeded in doing apart from Zaydi territory in the north. Another brother, after more fighting, succeeded in consolidating the Ayyubid state. The Ayyubids, 1173-1229, conquered the non-Zaydi areas of the Tihamah and the southern highlands. After the fall of the Ayyubids, one of its governors in Yemen, named Nur al-Din Umar ibn al-Rasul, founded the brilliant Rasulid dynasty. The Rasulids (1228-1454) built on the military successes of the Ayyubids: encouraged trade, administration, the arts, literature and education. Under al-Muzaffar Yusuf, they succeeded in controlling the whole of south-west Arabia and Hadhramaut and as far as Dhofar. The Zaydis controlled part of the country north of Sana'a. During the Rasulid period there was peace and stability. Trade flourished, especially through the port of Aden. During the Middle Ages dynasties rose and fell and ruled from different areas.

No account of the country through the Middle Ages would be complete without the rich source of material in the writings of Arab historians, philosophers and geographers, some of whom came from Yemen. To these Arab scholars, says Reynold Nicholson, author of *A Literary History of the Arabs*, 1930, a debt is owed as 'pioneers of learning and bringers of light to medieval Europe', adding: 'A chapter at least would be required in order to set forth adequately the chief material and intellectual benefits which European civilisation has derived from the Arabs.'

The Sultans of Turkey were ambitious to control the Red Sea route to India in order to extend their conquests eastward, and to endeavour to put an end to Portuguese depredations and render the sea routes safe during the pilgrimage to Mecca. The first Turkish occupation of Yemen began in the 1500s, during the reign of Suleiman the Magnificent (1520-66) when the Ottoman fleet captured Aden and some years later a Pasha was installed at Sana'a as Governor of Yemen. Turkish rule lasted a century. By the middle of the sixteenth century the Zaydis had become the strongest indigenous group. In 1569 a strong Turkish expeditionary force tried to establish its authority, but in the highlands they could achieve little. In 1590 a new Zaydi leader emerged who was to become a great hero, particularly as a result of his role in expelling the Turks. This was Qasim the Great, founder of the succession of Imams who ruled from Sana'a. Qasim was born in 1570 but was not descended from Ali ibn Abi Talib through Zayd and his grandfather, Husayn, but through Ali's other son, Hasan, the elder of the two. Seven of his ancestors had been Zaydi Imams. Turkish occupation was so detested that it aroused some spirit of unity in Yemen. The Turks were cruel, corrupt and immoral. This last counted most against them. A great preacher of that period said that the vice of sodomy had become so rampant amongst the Turkish soldiers and civilians at that time, that the people were compelled to screen their boys to the same extent as they screened their girls. Qasim grew up in an atmosphere of an increasing hatred of the Turks and, while this made him an ardent nationalist, it did not interfere with a natural inclination towards scholarship. When he was only twenty-seven, he was encouraged to proclaim himself Imam by his many supporters who recognised him as a great leader. His title was al-Mansur Billah ~ 'the Victorious by the Grace of God'. Qasim died in 1620. His son, al-Muayyad Mohammed, succeeded him and continued his father's campaign against corrupt and unjust rule. The Ottoman Empire grew weak, which affected its rule in Yemen: in 1629 Sana'a was surrendered.

The Zaydi Imamate was never purely hereditary. The Imam was elected from within a definite hereditary group. Any descendant of the Prophet Mohammed with the qualifications of piety, religious learning, generosity and administrative, military and political skills might claim the Imamate. The succession during the seventeenth and eighteenth centuries was often

A camel rider, believed to be a carrier of merchandise between Arabia and Egypt and dressed in a long tunic, faces the viewer and carries a spear in his right hand. The camel, with decorated neck band, walks proudly behind the cameleer, who wears a short tunic and also carries a spear in his right hand. Above the rider's head is an inscription from Marib.   *Bird*

fiercely contested and the *ulema*, learned men with the knowledge of Islamic law and traditions, played a decisive role. At times, the succession was decided by the sword. In the late seventeenth and early eighteenth centuries, rival Imams and chiefs soon arose. By 1728 the limits of the Imam's authority had greatly shrunk: Zaydi rule disappeared in Yafa', an old stronghold of Himyaritic power, and in Aulaqi country, to the east of Yafa'. In the same year the Imam's Governor of Lahej proclaimed himself an independent Sultan, and so Aden ceased to be part of the Imam's dominions. The Governor of Asir, a Sharif of lineage, also broke away in 1730. Hadhramaut had for long been virtually independent.

By 1763, little of the Tihamah remained under the rule of the Imam. The powerful Sharifs of Abu Arish in Asir continued extending their rule in the Tihamah until, by about 1790, the whole of the coast of Yemen from Qunfida to Bayt al-Faqih was occupied by them. Only in Mocha did the Imam's rule prevail.

There was contention between the different tribes of Hadhramaut as to which of them should ~ or could ~ control the inland settlements and ports, the principal contenders being Kathiri, Qu'aiti, Kasadi and Ahl Bureik. The Kathiri are believed to have originated in Dhofar and had been living in Hadhramaut. They were of little importance until they began to make themselves felt. In 1489, Sultan Abdullah bin Ja'fer al-Kathir became Governor of Shihr, but he did not live long, and in 1504 he was succeeded by his son Badr Bu Tuweirak bin Abdullah, who reigned for sixty years. This Kathiri leader was 'lord of Hadhramaut and Dhofar'. He proved to be a formidable adversary of both the Portuguese and the Turks.

The Qu'aiti, Kasadi and Ahl Bureik had originally come from their beautiful highland region of Yafa', to the west of Hadhramaut. The Yafa'i, known as Beni Himyar, Sons of Himyar traditionally descended from Qahtan, identified with the figure of Joktan in Genesis, who is said to have travelled to Hadhramaut in pre-Islamic times. Over the centuries, many of the clansmen established themselves throughout Hadhramaut and became very powerful. In the nineteenth century, struggle for control of inland and coastal settlements of Hadhramaut brought in the British who, until the 1860s, had only been interested in the activities of the tribes in the vicinity of Aden, which they had seized in 1839. Attempts by the Turks to annex Mukalla, Shihr and much of the south coast in 1850 and 1867 failed. The British became even more involved because the Qu'aiti ~ together with other Yafa'i ~ had been recruited into the army of the Nizam of Hyderabad, who wished to maintain his position in a predominantly Hindu state by bringing in tough, independent-minded Muslims. The principal Arab officers in the Nizam's service were known as jemadars. Because of the age-old trading links between Western India and South Arabia, a steady flow of adventurers from Hadhramaut to the service of Indian princes had been maintained. This connection, which had helped to make some of the leading Qu'aiti families rich and influential, induced the Prime Minister of Hyderabad to ask the Governor of Bombay to assist the Qu'aiti in Hadhramaut. The British were concerned that if the Qu'aiti were in control, the Nizam of Hyderabad's influence might jeopardize British interests. For this reason they, at first, supported the Kasadi. Eventually, the British acknowledged that the Qu'aiti were 'enlightened' and 'popular' ~ they also had essential administrative and leadership qualities and financial strength. The Kasadi Naqib, who had held Mukalla, left for Zanzibar with a pension. The Ahl Bureik had already been turned out of Shihr by the Kathiri, but now they ~ the Kathiri ~ had to be content with ruling only in Seiyun and Tarim in Wadi Hadhramaut, with no gateway to the sea. The Qu'aiti ruled in Mukalla, Shihr and important inland towns, notably Shibam in Wadi Hadhramaut.

In 1882 the Qu'aiti Sultan Abdullah bin Umar bin Awadh, on behalf of himself and his brother, Awadh bin Umar, signed a treaty with the British by which he agreed to accept advice in dealing with outside powers and not to cede or to mortgage any part of his land to anyone other than the British. This was followed in 1888 with a full Protectorate Treaty with the same clauses. Thirty years later a Qu'aiti-Kathiri Agreement was signed, by which the Kathiri Sultan of Seiyun and Tarim, Mansur bin Ghalib, agreed to accept as binding the treaty of 1888 between the Qu'aiti and the British Government. The Kathiri also accepted the arbitration of the British Government in the settlement of future disputes. Thus the whole of Hadhramaut came into the orbit of what became known as the Aden Protectorate.

Foreign travellers to Yemen came not only as merchant adventurers and traders, they also came on important exploratory and scientific expeditions and missions. Benjamin of Tudela, a Spanish rabbi, may have sailed there on his journey from Basra to Egypt *circa* 1170. He referred to Aden as 'Eden' or 'Middle India'. He wrote that many independent tribes of Jews lived in the mountains and survived by plundering their Muslim neighbours. In the thirteenth century, the Venetian traveller, Marco Polo, stopped in Aden *en route* to China. The celebrated Moroccan, Mohammed bin Abdullah ibn Battuta, pilgrim and traveller, left Tangier, his birthplace, in June 1325 with the intention of making the pilgrimage to Mecca. He left Mecca at the end of 1330 to journey through Yemen and beyond.

Trade with China flourished in the eleventh, twelfth and thirteenth centuries. 'Chau ju-kua of the Sung dynasty', while holding the post of inspector of foreign taxes in Fukien, used the accounts brought back by eye-witnesses and described how the Chinese traded with the Arabs. Between 1405 and 1433 the Chinese again took an interest in South Arabia. The illustrious Admiral Cheng-ho made seven voyages of discovery in the Indian Ocean. Had the Chinese persisted in their trading ventures, the Portuguese would have found them powerful rivals, as they were better equipped, and their fleet, consisting of 62 ships and 28,000 men, was far larger.

In May 1487 King John II of Portugal sent Pedro da Covilham on a voyage of exploration in the Levant, Asia and Africa to discover where 'cinnamon and other spices could be found' and to reach Ethiopia ~ 'the land of Prester John', which he did in 1490. In his travels from Cairo to India and back he touched several times at Aden. In 1505 Diego Fernandes Pereira, the captain of a ship then patrolling off the African coast, was forced to shelter at Socotra during the monsoon period and conveyed the earliest Portuguese report on the island to Dom Manuel I, King of Portugal.

From 1500 to 1800 the Portuguese were not the only Europeans to contribute substantially to the course of events in the Indian Ocean and the Red Sea: the English, Dutch, French and Danish, and the Americans, also visited the area. During this period a substantial number of engravings were struck which portray the different aspects of Yemen. Throughout the eighteenth century the English and the Dutch, until the latter departed, had control of Yemen's foreign trade. Yemeni coffee went to all parts of the world and coffee houses sprang up all over Europe. The Americans, too, came for the coffee, but they also traded in cotton goods ~ a trade that once flourished between Salem, in Massachusetts, and the Red Sea ports. The American cloth, known in Yemen as *mericani*, arrived in its natural colour, was then dyed with indigo and bought extensively by bedouin who wound it around their bodies as a *futah*, using another length to cover their shoulders and heads as protection against the cold of the desert at night. Early European merchant seamen did not all come to trade legitimately, indeed during the seventeenth century the Indian Ocean was swarming with European pirates. 'They were not, normally, protected by the European governments ... and the Muslim rulers were hopelessly confused about the relations of the different nations of Europe', wrote the noted twentieth century scholar, Charles Beckingham.

In 1798 Napoleon invaded Egypt and overthrew the Mamluk sultans, vassals of the Ottoman Caliph. The British saw this as a threat to their communications with India and occupied the island of Perim (Mayun) in the straits of Bab al-Mandab in 1799. Since the island had no sweet water the troops withdrew to Aden where they were hospitably received by the Abdali Sultan of Lahej. The Sultan's territory expanded in the south to the peninsula of Aden and its port, with which he kept contact along a narrow funnel of land between the territories of the Fadhli and Aqrabi tribes. He offered Aden to the British, but the offer was not accepted.

The rise to power in Egypt of Mohammed Ali Pasha, an Albanian soldier who was made Viceroy of Egypt by the Ottoman Sultan, posed a dilemma for the makers of British policy in the Red Sea. They were determined that no other power should establish itself in the area. Mohammed Ali was warned not to pass Bab al-Mandab nor to touch Aden. During the campaigns in Yemen under his nephew, Ibrahim Pasha, the British Government, according to a Foreign Office memorandum, 'treated the proceedings of Ibrahim Pasha the younger as an occupation only'.

The introduction of steam navigation led the Bombay Government to send two survey vessels to the Red Sea in order to facilitate navigation, to ensure the safety of steam ships, and to promote rapid communication. There was also the important question of finding coaling depôts to fuel the hungry boilers of the steam vessels on the India-Suez route. In 1828 a coaling station was established at Mocha and in 1829 coal was landed on Sira Island, off Aden, and also along the coast at Mukalla. Various places were considered as suitable stations, including Socotra island, and it was decided to occupy Socotra which proved to be disastrous, mainly because of the unhealthy climate. In January 1837 an Indian ship under British colours was plundered off Aden. The Sultan of Lahej seems to have been implicated and, since negotiations for compensation proved unsatisfactory, Captain Haines of the Indian Navy was ordered to enforce the cession of Aden in consideration of an annual payment to the Sultan of 8,700 Maria Theresa dollars. This came to nothing. A British expedition arrived off Aden in January 1839. In order to land forces to capture the town it was necessary first to silence the Arab guns on the well-fortified island of Sira ~ the effective

Mohammed Ali Pasha. *MassajaII.93.*

defence through Aden's history against invaders, but Sira was stormed by the British and they took Aden. Around 1,000 Arabs fought to resist the attack.

On 19 January 1839 the British flag was hoisted on the Sultan of Lahej's palace and a flag of truce on the mosque dedicated to Sayyid Aidrous, patron saint of Aden. Many attempts to retake Aden were made by the Arabs. Sultan Muhsin bin Fadhl al-Abdali used his wealth to form one coalition after another to oust the British from his port, but his forces were repulsed. The Bombay Government accused Haines of being too hard on the Sultan. It urged him to conclude peace with the Sultan and to show a more conciliatory attitude towards him. A letter from the Sultan reminded Haines: 'I have lost everything: you have Aden.' Mohammed Ali tried to persuade the Imam to turn out the British, but this, the Imam declared, was impossible, and Aden became a dependency of India, with Captain Stafford Bettesworth Haines as its first Political Agent.

Between 1849-50 and 1872 when the Turks captured Sana'a there were years of anarchy and various claimants to the Imamate. In 1879 al-Hadi Sharaf al-Din proclaimed himself Imam. After his death in 1890 al-Mansur billah Mohammed bin Yahya Hamid al-Din was recognised as the new Imam. He died in 1904. Yemen was considered to be a *vilayet* with a *wali* and *mutasarrifs* ruling administrative districts after the Turks took Sana'a. The whole country was now occupied by two powers. The delimitation of a boundary between the Turkish-controlled north and the British-occupied south: Aden Settlement (Colony in 1937) and the Aden Protectorate (Western and Eastern Aden Protectorates in 1937) ~ divided Yemen into two geographical and political units. This division was never accepted by the Arabs who had taken no part in the demarcation of the Anglo-Turkish Line (instituted in 1902-4 and ratified in 1914). After the signing of the armistice, the evacuation of the Turks began, although some remained and were absorbed into Yemeni society. A notable, Mohammed Raghib Bey, who had served in the Ottoman diplomatic service before the

1914-18 war, acted as Adviser on Foreign Affairs to Imam Yahya (1904-1948). The British occupation of the South lasted until the end of November 1967.

The illustrations selected for this volume are designed to present, where possible, an in-depth view of Yemen and are therefore drawn from a wide range of sources irrespective of the technical processes employed. As is evident from the illustrations, Yemen is a breathtakingly beautiful country and is extraordinarily varied: strikingly high mountains, many with terrace upon terrace, deftly carved into the mountain sides, reaching the summit; deep chasms with waterfalls, and lush vegetation where birds and other wildlife abound; ever-changing sand dunes in the desert at the southern tip of the Empty Quarter and the coast; awe-inspiring plateaux baked by the sun, and intersected by deep abysses, bright green with date gardens and different cultivation, which line the bottom, and mud-brick houses 'slide down' the valley walls. Famed for their inspiring architecture, some of Yemen's cities and towns have been classed as world heritage sites by UNESCO. The Red Sea and south coasts change from mountains disappearing into the sea to sandy beaches that stretch as far as the eye can see. Rugged peaks of drowned mountain ranges appear on the surface of the sea as rocky islands and islets with little vegetation. Then there is the 'Isle of the Blest', Socotra, incomparable in its flora and fauna. In July 2003 the Socotra Archipelago was given important recognition by UNESCO as a 'Man and Biosphere Reserve' ~ the first of its kind in Yemen or the Arabian Peninsula. Scientists and other scholars are currently working on the designation of the Socotran Archipelago as a World Heritage Site. It is also part of a new 'hotspot' ~ the whole Horn of Africa area ~ designated by Conservation International.

The official language of Yemen is Arabic. Two quite different languages are unwritten: Mahri in Mahra and in Socotra a related language, Socotri. Travellers and scholars over the years have recorded and studied different aspects of these unwritten languages, including their folklore and poetry. The capital of present-day Yemen is Sana'a ~ the cultural capital of the Arab World in 2004. Aden is the economic and commercial capital. Yemen has nineteen governorates and its population is over 18 million. The country has been a magnet to travellers for thousands of years, from the days of its reputed wealth through the trade in frankincense and myrrh and because of its strategic position on the southwest corner of the peninsula of Arabia ~ linking east and west. Foreigners have settled in the country. Also the people, for various reasons, have migrated East and West and some returned with foreign spouses to their beloved country. The country therefore, as several engravings bear witness, is inhabited by an inter-blending of diverse peoples with differing physical features, cultures, dress, traditional housing, economic activities and way of life

Yemen and Ethiopia, two great civilisations, have been linked commercially and historically for thousands of years, and by land in prehistoric times. *Yemen Engraved* is a sister book to *Ethiopia Engraved* by Richard Pankhurst and myself. *Ethiopia Engraved* included detailed portraits of emperors and leading notables. During much of the period covered in *Yemen Engraved*, it was frowned upon and even prohibited to depict the human form, hence the scarcity of engravings of rulers and notables in this book. Therefore some captions are unusually long, quoting the travellers' text, in order to describe notables who are not clearly depicted. This volume ends in the nineteenth century, therefore any pictorial sequel will be told in the medium of photography. During the photographic period, a good many photographs of rulers and notables were taken.

The Yemenis, in the last analysis, have their enduring and unique culture, and are proud of their rich heritage and ancient history. They are among the most friendly and most hospitable people in the world.

1

LANDSCAPE & ARCHITECTURE

'The early morning effect upon the flat plateau was one of great beauty. As we proceeded the cultivated land became very sparse ... we entered a great circular plain enclosed by low rocky hills on all sides. From this point one catches a glimpse of Jebel Doran, a range of mountains of great elevation which terminate in a strange sugar loaf peak.' *Harris 282*

Mountains & Valleys

A village in Wadi Khoreiba, on the road from Aden to Sana'a. *Harris 213*

Left: A peaceful scene in Khoreiba with great, bare rocky mountains forming a backdrop. *Harris 193*

Above: A gigantic rock and a tree form a natural arch over a camel caravan route through the mountains. *Manzoni 38*

Above: Steep steps lead to the stone houses of a mountain village. *Manzoni 57*

Left: Watering camels in the valley. Azab, north of Qataba, is 'perched on the very summit of a high hill, and a confusion of walls and towers'. *Harris 218*

Below: At the very edge of the chasms, stone houses stand upright as if to guard the cultivated terraces, near Suq al-Khamis, between Hodeidah and Sana'a. Such chasms often served a defensive purpose. *Harris* 18

Near the south coast the landscape is mountainous with numerous fertile valleys, producing cotton-trees, coffee, wheat and millet in abundance, and were carpeted with water melons, the size of a man's head. Yafa' spreads over an extensive area, reaching some 6,500 feet above sea level.

Above left is the village of Jowalah, and, on the *right*, Teran, with British camp. Al-Salih is pictured *below*. In the early 1830s, during his survey of the south coast, Captain Haines of the Indian Navy, wrote of Al-Salih: 'It contains 200 houses, 40 of which are built of stone – its population about 500; the country immediately around is well watered and cultivated ... To the South East of Al-Salih is the tomb of a Sheikh.' *ILN.*

Above: **Dhamar (south of Sana'a), at the end of the nineteenth century, with its stone houses, forms 'a city of science and art'.** *Manzoni 83*

Left: **A flight of steps descends to the water's edge at one of the ancient water cisterns near Dhamar, where cameleers quench their thirst. Camels and other animals drink from a separate cistern.** *Harris 38*

Left: 'The town of Manakha is quite a small one. It contains, perhaps, some five thousand inhabitants, without counting the very considerable number of Turkish troops stationed there at the time of my visit [1890s]. The houses are well built of stone, some of them four storeys, and many three, in height'. The town is situated 'some seven thousand six hundred feet above the sea-level' and it dominates 'the two parts of the highroad from Hodaidah to Sanaa.' The bazaar 'is tolerably well supplied with the necessaries of life, though at the time of my visit meat and vegetables were scarce, on account of the influx of [Turkish] troops.' One or two of the shops were kept by Greeks.   *Harris 110*

In the early 1890s, Walter Harris remarked: 'Of all the places it has ever been my lot to see, Manakha is the most wonderfully situated. The town is perched on a narrow strip of mountain that joins two distinct ranges, and it forms the watershed of two great valleys ... So narrow is the ridge on which the town stands, that the walls of the houses on both sides seem almost to hang over the precipices.

'As our road proceeded it increased in magnificence, entering the heart of the mountains, on the summit of one of which the town of Manakha is perched ... we gazed at the scene before us. Wonderful, stupendous it was!'

Right: Turkish soldiers camp on the ledge below Manakha and a Turkish soldier stands guard in front.   *Harris 322*

Left: View near Wisil, south of Manakha. 'wonderfully perched on the very edge of the precipice' in magnificent surroundings.
Harris 342

Below: 'The remarkable village of Kariat al-Hajra near Manakha, a rock crowned with tall stone houses, many of which are built in the strange fashion of towers. A precipice surrounds the village on every side, the lower slopes of which are cultivated in terraces.'
Harris 342

Above: Bayt al-Nedish, south of Yarim, 'standing on the very edge of high precipices, presents a most picturesque appearance. In the centre rises a high tower, the largest of these solidly built Arab burj we had as yet come across.' A graveyard lies to the right.
Harris 226

Above: **Qarat al-Negil, south of Sana'a, 'its very rock crowned by stone towers – a striking and wild-looking place,' overlooks the terraces below.** *Harris 262*

Above: **Khadar, north of Qarat al-Negil, is picturesque 'though greatly lacking in vegetation ... the inhabitants are almost entirely Jews.'** *Harris 286*

Right: **A bedouin and his couched camel in Wadi Khoreiba. Standing on the summit of a 'high rock loomed the frontier fort of the Amir of Dhala ... the river, dancing and rippling over its pebbly bed ... around it twined masses of flowering creepers and strange aloes, while a palm-tree here and there raised its feathery head above the dense undergrowth'.** *Harris 195*

Above: **The town of Yarim in the early 1760s surrounds the hill fort, its mosque stands on the outskirts to the right.** *Niebuhr(2)I.Pl.LXVIII*

Below: **The castle of the Fadhli sultan dominates Khanfar, in Fadhli territory.** *Bent(1)402*

Below: **Houses of Hadhramaut, with wooden screen windows and ventilation apertures above them, as described to L.W.C. van den Berg by Hadhramis living in the Dutch East Indies, 1880s.** *Berg end*

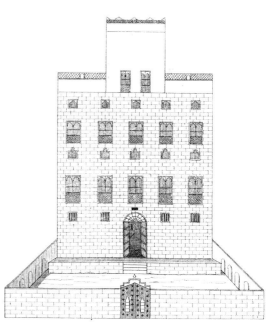

Above: **A laden camel is led past the domed tombs of saints at al-Gheidha, Mahra, in 1836**. *NicholsonPl.VI*

Below: **The picturesque gateway of a walled village with steps, flanked by two turrets, leading to upper rooms.** *Harris 354*

Below: **A house in Mahra in 1836, with four ventilation apertures above the level of the windows and door. In the foreground, a man is feeding a goat.** *NicholsonPl.I*

Mosques & Minarets

Right: North of Shuqra, old Na'ab, Wadi Yaramis in Fadhli country: 'We soon burst upon a lovely plain all mapped out in fields .... This cultivated paradise is the property of Sultan Ahmet bin Salem, brother to Sultan Saleh on the coast.' The mosque and minaret, 'and a fine old house all tumbling into ruins.' Mrs. Bent wrote in the early 1890s: 'Our party was now increased by another "prince", Sultan Haidar, son of the Sultan of Na'ab, a person delightful to contemplate. He was got up in Bedou style; his hair, fluffy and long, was tied back by a fillet and stuck out in a bush behind. He was wrapped in a couple of large blue cotton cloths with very long fringes. The cotton is plastered with indigo. The richer you are the bluer you are, and Sultan Haidar was very blue indeed.'   *Bent 413*

Above: 'A pretty little white mosque' at Bayt Said, south of Yarim, flanked by trees.   *Harris 232*

Below: A Hadhrami mosque and minaret in Wadi Hadhramaut, described in the 1880s to van den Berg by Hadhramis living in the Dutch East Indies.   *Berg end*

Below: The mosque and minaret at Dhamar; in the foreground the men engage in commerce and conversation. *Harris 259*

2

SANA'A & TA'IZZ

A minaret and decorated façade of a stone house in Sana'a at the end of the 1870s. Round windows made of alabaster give a moonlight effect to a room, hence the name in Arabic, *qamariyyah*. The apertures above and on each side of the entrance give air and light to the ground floor and stairs.   *Manzoni 120*

'Sana'a be it must, however long the journey', comes from a traditional poem cited by the tenth century South Arabian scholar al-Hamdani, and others. Al-Hamdani remarked that Sana'a 'is regarded by all people as one of the gardens of the earth'.

Spreading out over a fertile elevated plain at the foot of Jebel Nuqum, Sana'a, the capital of Yemen, occupies a site that stands on a major ancient north-south route. Pre-Islamic inscriptions indicate that Sana'a was important as a dynastic and military headquarters. According to local legends it was founded by Noah's son, Shem, and it is said to be one of the oldest continuously inhabited cities of the world. The famous Ghumdan was a palace said to be twenty storeys high with four bronze lions on its roof which roared when the wind blew. Another of the glories of ancient Sana'a was the cathedral, al-Qalis, called after the Greek word for church, *eklesia*, which was built by Abraha, the Ethiopian, who conquered Yemen in AD 525. Al-Hamdani writes of the Ghumdan, as eulogised by earlier poets and writers, but of which nothing existed in his time except for some of the lower sections of the wall. During his visit to Sana'a in the early 1890s, Walter Harris, *The Times* correspondent, saw that 'nothing but a heap of ruins remains' of the 'palace and temple'.

Sana'a's early Islamic history began in AD 622 with Islam itself. Early historians report that the Great Mosque was built on the order of the Prophet Mohammed during his lifetime. Possibly only a few fragments now remain of that Great Mosque.

The old city stands within its ancient walls of sun-dried brick and at its western end is crossed by a dry watercourse which was spanned by a stone bridge used in the time of flood. Abdul Rahman ibn Zayd ibn Khaldun, the renowned fourteenth century scholar, who was born in Tunis, but who traced his origins to Hadhramaut, called Sana'a 'the most celebrated city of Yaman'. The high square houses of the old city are striking, and many visitors have been impressed by them. In 1510, Ludovico di Varthema, a 'gentleman of the Citie of Rome', gives us the first written account by a European, noting that the houses are of 'fayre building … The citie is so large, that it conteyneth within the walles, fields, gardens and medowes.'

The German, Carsten Niebuhr, accompanied by the other survivors of a Danish mission, arrived in Sana'a in July 1763. In keeping with strict etiquette, Niebuhr and his party were prevented from making or receiving visits until they had paid their respects to Imam Abbas bin Husayn. On the third day after their arrival in Sana'a the party was invited to an audience with him. Niebuhr explored the city and found its markets and

magnificent buildings a very paradise. He described the 'great simseras or caravanserais for merchants and travellers ... In the market for bread, none but women are to be seen; and their little shops are portable ... Writers go about with their desks, and make out brieves, copy-books and instruct scholars in the art of writing, all at the same time.' Niebuhr visited the communities of the Jews of Qa'al-Yahud, of which he estimated the population was 2,000, and of the Indian traders, of which he guessed there were 125. He attempted to draw a map of Sana'a although he found it difficult to be accurate because of the curious and excited inhabitants surrounding him. He was fortunate to watch the Imam return from his Friday devotions, attended by the princes and followed by hundreds of soldiers. A parasol, the emblem of royalty, sheltered him from the sun and on each side was borne a standard 'having upon it a small silver box filled with amulets, whose efficacy was imagined to render him invincible … The riders paced or galloped, at pleasure, and all went in confusion.'

Nearly seventy years later, Lt. Charles Cruttenden of the Indian Navy visited Sana'a in the reign of Ali bin Abdullah al-Mansur. 'The Imam of Sana'a', he wrote, 'has two large palaces with extensive gardens adjoining; the whole walled round and fortified'. Cruttenden remarks that 'Fountains appear to be indispensable in the houses at Sana'a, and in the Bustan el-Mutawakkil [one of the palaces] there are several. The Imam has a stud of very fine horses.' He adds that Sana'a has 'perhaps 40,000' inhabitants. 'On Friday the Imam goes in state to the mosque, and the procession we witnessed was very splendid'. The Imam, dressed superbly, sat on a magnificent white charger. 'He held in his hand a long spear with a silver head, having the shaft gilt. His left hand rested on the shoulder of a confidential eunuch, and two grooms led his horse. A very magnificent canopy, much like an umbrella in form, was carried over his head, having the fringe ornamented with silver bells.'

In April 1872 Sana'a came under Turkish rule once again. Turkish troops were stationed in Ta'izz and the Political Resident Aden, eager to learn of their movements, sent a special messenger to Ta'izz who returned to Aden with the

Panorama of the walled city of Sana'a, as seen from the Governor's house at the end of the 1870s. Renzo Manzoni likened the bastions, supporting the city walls, to enormous puddings. *Manzoni 187*

The castle dominates the walled city of Ta'izz on the lower slopes of Jebel Sabir.
Niebuhr(2)I.Pl.LXVII

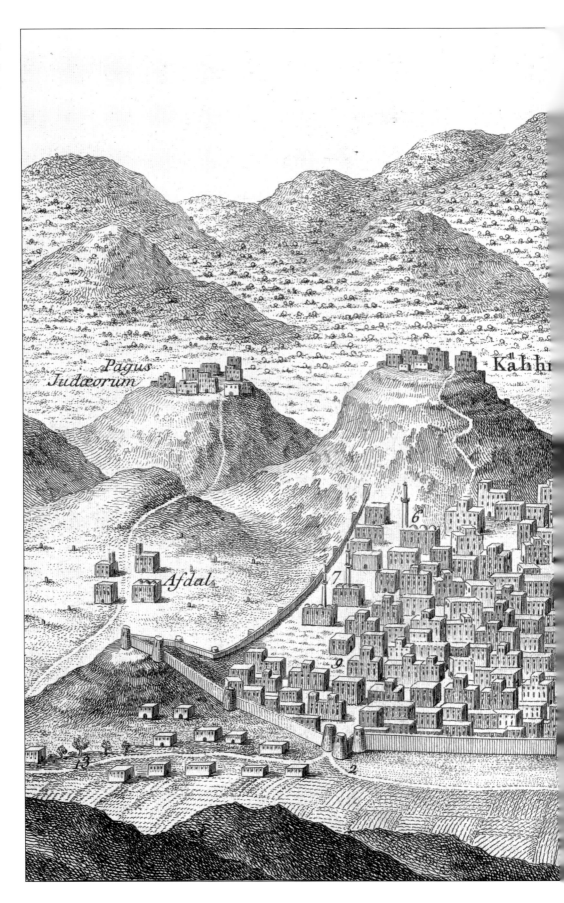

following intelligence which was forwarded to the Secretary to the Government of Bombay on 24 January 1873: 'On arriving at Ta'izz he [the special messenger] found that the Turkish soldiers were on guard at every gate in the town, and that they were busily engaged in repairing the fortifications and in erecting new defensive works ... he also saw the whole of the garrison on parade, and states that the three regiments present did not comprise less than 2,000 men.'

The Italian traveller, Renzo Manzoni, visited between October 1877 and February 1880, and wandered through Sana'a and thought it very clean and beautiful, although it was full of dogs. Cruttenden, he felt, had exaggerated its population and estimated that there were only about 20,000 Arabs, 3,000 Turks, 1,700 Jews and one Greek pharmacist. Manzoni witnessed an enormous flood in August 1878, when more than one hundred houses were damaged. He related the changes taking place in this city under Turkish rule: there was a magnificent hospital, a school which gave technical education, and a weekly postal service and telegraphic link to Hodeidah, on the Red Sea Coast.

North Yemen remained under Turkish rule until the end of the First World War. Some fine buildings were constructed during the Turkish occupations, and there were changes in the administration of the city. Manzoni just saw the great barracks, Dar Sabro, built during the first Turkish occupation, 'in pure and rich Arab style' before they were demolished by Mustapha Asim Pasha in 1878. The stairs had been so well constructed in the nine-storey building that the favourite white donkey of the Commandant was able to climb to its stall on the sixth floor. Some years later, the British correspondent, Walter Harris, too visited Sana'a, and wrote that the whole town was surrounded by a wall which the Turks fortified at regular intervals by building towers 'somewhat resembling our martello towers' and erected guns upon the main wall. Included in the fine buildings were al-Muradiyyah mosque and, in particular, al-Bakiriyyah mosque completed by the Ottoman Hasan Pasha in 1596-8, who had also built the public baths, Hammam al-Maydan, at about the same time.

In the reign of the self-proclaimed Imam, al-Hadi Sharaf al-Din, Shaykh Ali bin Mohammed al-Bilayli al-Sanani, Mayor of Sana'a and founder of the mosque named after him, was deposed in 1887-88 by the incoming Turkish Governor, Othman Nuri Pasha. Othman Nuri appointed a Turk, Mustapha Effendi al-Qaysarli. The new mayor made several administrative changes during the years 1887-8. He regulated the affairs of the city and fixed the weights and measures in the markets. By his order the streets and lanes were to be cleaned and the use of obscene language was forbidden. A decade later, Husayn Hilmi Pasha, another Turkish Governor and a man of learning, modernised Sana'a. He founded a number of educational institutions and built the Dar al-Wilayah. The Majlis Idarat al-Wilayah, the Provincial Administrative Council, was set up to review the affairs of the Province. A law which laid down that

Right: **Characteristic houses of Sana'a. The ground floor of a Sanani house is reserved for animals and timber storage, the first is for grain storage. Strangers are received on the second floor rooms, in which there are often projected wooden-screened windows where water jars are stood to keep cool. The third floor is usually for the main family room and other living rooms, and the kitchen is above, so that it can serve the rooms below. The room on top is used for afternoon entertainment of guests, to chew *qat* and to relax.** *Manzoni 90*

Sana'a – 'the much-bedomed Turkish mosque', al-Bakiriyyah, built by the Ottoman governor,
Hasan Pasha. He named it after a client of his, Bakir Bey, who was thrown from his horse
during cavalry games in Sana'a. The minaret is in the traditional Yemeni style.   *Harris 316*

Arab officials serving with the Turks were to wear Turkish clothing caused great
offence to the Yemenis. Some years later, Husayn Hilmi Pasha rescinded this law and
Yemeni officials reverted to wearing Arab clothing.

   To the south of Sana'a lies Ta'izz on the lowest spur of its majestic green
mountain, Jebel Sabir. Intricate terraces, carved into its sides to the very top, hold
rainwater as it pours down, irrigating Yemen crops and overflowing from one terrace to
the next. The remains of a castle at its peak are said to be pre-Islamic. The fortress
of al-Qahirah crowns a precipitous detached crag which dominates the city from
the southeast. In the spring of 1763, Niebuhr and his party journeyed to Ta'izz. He

refers to the fortress as 'Kahhre', stating that it 'stands in the circuit of the [city] wall'. Mount Sabir had the reputation locally of being covered with 'plants of every species that is to be found anywhere else through the world. Mr. Forskal [botanist on the Danish expedition, who died at Yarim] had this mountain daily before his eyes, but, to his infinite mortification, could not obtain permission to botanize upon it.' The governor refused Forskal permission to visit Sabir because he was at war with a tribe in that district.

Ta'izz has been beautified both by local dynasties and by outsiders who have conquered Yemen. It became the seat of the splendid Rasulid dynasty. The Rasulids (1228-1454) unified most of historic Yemen. Nur al-Din Umar ibn al-Rasul, the founder of this remarkable dynasty, conducted an active foreign policy, driving the Egyptians from Mecca and establishing relations with the Caliphs of Baghdad. The Rasulid court historian, Ali bin al-Hasan al-Khazraji, author of *The Pearl Strings (al-Uqud al-lu'lu'iyyah)*, speaks highly of Nur al-Din, Umar ibn al-Rasul: 'a noble, prudent, clement prince, excellent in governing, quick in action in an emergency'. He adds that in 1232 Nur al-Din commanded 'money to be coined in his name, and he also ordered the preachers to offer public prayer for him in every region of Yemen.' He began an active policy of building: erecting a mosque in every village of the Tihamah and religious academies with rich endowments in Ta'izz, Zabid and Aden. The

Houses and gardens inside the walls of the city of Sana'a. A covered well in the centre from which the women have collected water. *Manzoni 124*

Rasulids expanded the city of Ta'izz greatly: magnificent mosques, colleges and palaces were built during their reign. The two most magnificent mosques, al-Ashrafiyya and al-Muzaffar, are named after Sultans al-Ashraf and al-Muzaffar.

Al-Muzaffar Yusuf (1249-1295), a skilled physician and scholar, continued his father's activities; his foreign policy was so active that al-Khazraji claimed that 'the hearts of the Princes of Persia and the lords of India and China were filled with fear when they saw his ambition and power.' In 1279, al-Muzaffar launched a well co-ordinated campaign against the ruler of Dhofar who had raided Aden.

The daughter of Nur al-Din, an exceptional person, was a 'wise, virtuous, prudent, intelligent woman, who loved her brother Mudhaffar most affectionately', wrote al-Khazraji. 'She was a dispenser of alms and charity, and many are the institutions she left behind her. Among them is the college known as the Shamsiyya, in Dhu Udeyna, a part of the city of Taiz, which is well-endowed in mortmain trust for a precentor, a mu'ezzin, a beadle, a professor, students, a teacher, and orphans to learn the Qur'an.'

Ibn Khaldun wrote in the fourteenth century that Ta'izz 'has always been one of the royal strongholds'. In this same century, the noted Moroccan traveller, ibn Battuta, wrote of 'the capital of the king of Yemen' as 'one of the finest towns in that country. Taiz is made up of three quarters: the first is the residence of the king and his court, the second called Udayna, is the military station, and the third, called al-Mahalib, is inhabited by the commanalty, and contains the principal market.' He describes the 'elaborate ceremonial' Nur al-Din Ali uses in his

Jebel Nuqum overlooks Sana'a in the east. In modern times, the eastern end of Sana'a climbs up the slopes of the mountain. Shining black stone from Nuqum was said to have been used in the building of al-Qalis, the famous cathedral of Sana'a built by Abraha, the Ethiopian.

Carsten Niebuhr wrote that ruins of a castle were still to be seen which, he said, the Arabs supposed had been built by Shem, the son of Noah. He added that aqueducts from Jebel 'Nikkim' supplied an abundance of fresh water. On the right are stables with horses and on the left, a well and cultivation. *Manzoni 166*

audiences and progresses 'The qadi presented me to him and I saluted him. The way in which one is to touch the ground with the index finger, then lift it to the head to say "May God prolong thy Majesty". I did as the qadi had done, and the king, having ordered me to sit in front of him, questioned me about my country and the other lands and princes I had seen.'

The Englishman, John Jourdain, on his pioneering journey to Yemen, arrived in Ta'izz in June 1609 and lodged in a 'faire sarraye' for three days. He wrote that Ta'izz was as big or bigger than Sana'a, lying on the side of a mountain with a 'very faire castell' on its top. He mentions 'many Turks soldiers, Ta'izz being one of the best and strongest cites in Arabia, with manie faire buildings of stone … and much trade with the Banians of Guzarrat.'

In 1837, the Imam's uncle, Sayyid Qasim, sold Ta'izz to the Egyptians, but their power did not last long. In 1840 they evacuated Yemen. Imam Ahmed resumed his old residence in Ta'izz from 1948, after the murder in Sana'a of his father, Imam Yahya, until his death in 1962. He rarely visited the capital, Sana'a.

Top storeys of a house in Bir al-Azab commanding splendid views over Sana'a and beyond.
Niebuhr(2)I.Pl.LXVIII

Above: Palace of the Imam of Sana'a, drawn by Lt Charles Cruttenden, in the 1830s. *Graphic*

Below: The walls of Sana'a, drawn by Lt Charles Cruttenden, in the 1830s. *Graphic*

3
ADEN & LAHEJ

A camel caravan reaches the top of the hill leading to the *aqaba* between Ma'alla and the volcanic crater at Aden (detail). *BernatzPl.II.*

Whatever its origins, there is no doubt that to the ancient mariners and to the Arabs of south-west Arabia, Aden was long regarded as the 'Eye of the Yemen', the organ through which the outside world was seen and through which foreign contacts were made. By its situation and formation it seems indeed to have been destined as fortress, harbour and market place. Its fortunes fluctuated through the centuries between prosperity and deprivation. Named 'Eudaemon Arabia' [Happy Arabia, as in Arabia Felix] and described as 'a village by the shore, having convenient anchorages and watering places' in the *Periplus of the Erythraean Sea*, by the time the Venetian Marco Polo came there in the 13th century it was a 'port to which many of the ships of India come with their cargoes, and from this haven the merchants carry the goods a distance of seven days further in small vessels [up the Red Sea].'

A century later, ibn Battuta, the Moroccan traveller, called Aden the 'Marsa', or anchorage. He wrote of the merchants of Aden being 'immensely rich, so rich that sometimes a single merchant is sole owner of a large ship with all it contains, and this is

Sira Island, the sentinel of Aden *circa* 1680, defending the town behind.   Dapper 28

a subject of ostentation and rivalry between them. In spite of that they are pious, humble, upright and generous in character, treat strangers well, and give liberally to devotees, and pay in full tithes due to God.'

The Portuguese merchant adventurer, Duarte Barbosa, was impressed by Aden. He arrived in 1518, at the 'populous and wealthy city ... which belongs to the Moors and has its own King. This city has a right good haven and an exceeding great traffic in goods of importance. It is a fine town, with lofty houses of stone and mortar, flat-roofed, with many tall windows; it is well laid out in streets and surrounded with walls, towers and bastions, with battlements after our fashion.' Travellers admired the magnificent backdrop to Aden – the mountain range of Mansuri, the highest mountain of which is Jebel Shamsan, dramatically depicted in engravings by early artists with 'small castles, very fair to behold' on the peaks. Writing in the early 1600s, the Englishman John Jourdain described the city after it was 'ruined and destroyed by the Turks', though there were still traces of its former glory.

With its natural defence in its mountain range and strategic position to become a prosperous trading centre, Aden lacked the one essential for survival – sweet water. A Persian ruler, locally referred to as Shah bin Jamshid, is credited with the construction of the celebrated Tanks in Tawilah gorge during the Persian occupation of the late sixth and seventh cenuries, although a much earlier date has also been considered. There are now eighteen tanks with a capacity of 10 million gallons. When they fill to overflowing, the water cascades down the gulleys into the top tank, then overflows from one into another. In the first decade of the nineteenth century, the distinguished British draftsman, Henry Salt, believed the Tanks to be the most remarkable remains in Aden. He noted that there was also a handsome terrace, behind which rose immense masses of granite, 'which being in some parts perpendicular, and in others overhanging it forms during the hot weather a most delightful retreat.' As the Tanks depend on rainwater they were an uncertain source of supply and it was necessary to find other ways to solve the problem of supplying sweet water. An early Arab ruler ordered that an aqueduct be laid from 'a distant place' and that a cistern be built on the piece of flat ground below Jebel Hadid in Ma'alla to receive the water. Salt saw the remains of both cistern and aqueduct which he said could be traced for about eight miles. He dated both after 1530 as he quoted a passage from a tract written in that year which said that water was brought in daily by some 1,500 to 2,000 camels. Desalinated water became another source of supply in 1869, when a plant was built on Sira Island.

Sira Island stands away from Sahel Abyan like a sentinel guarding the approaches to Aden, which indeed it did during the centuries when foreign invaders sought to conquer it. 'On the day of Judgement', declared ibn al-Mujawir, the thirteenth century traveller, 'fire will be emitted from the Sira of Aden and drive the people to hell and the proof of that is, that in the heart of the rock is a well named Amber, and smoke issues from it perpetually. No one is able to look at it on account of its terribleness and its gloom and vapour'. Could this be some handed down memory of volcanic Aden? It has been said that, if being of pure heart and simple faith, you climb to the top of the island at midnight when the moon is full, and look across the bay into the desert, you will see the fair and wondrous city of Iram dhat al-Imad (Iram of the Columns). Sheddad, the son of Ad, is said to have ordered a terrestrial paradise to be built in the desert of Aden to rival the celestial one, and called it Iram after his great-grandfather. This was the 'Iram of the Columns, the like of which has not been created in these lands', according to the chapter *The Dawn* of the *Qur'an*. On going to take possession of his wondrous city Sheddad was struck dead together with all his people by a

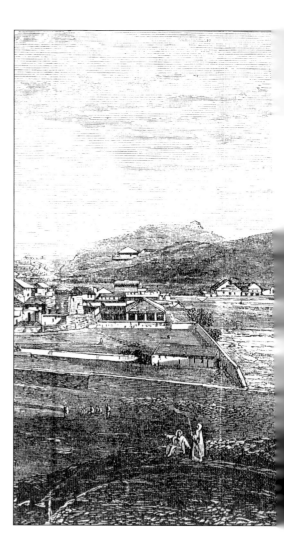

Contemporary portrait of Afonso d'Albuquerque.
Felner Frontispiece.

terrible, violent wind. So Sheddad never saw his paradise, 'and since Sheddad nobody has seen it', according to the ninth century historian Abu Ja'far Mohammed al-Tabari.

Ludovico di Varthema, the early sixteenth century Italian traveller, noted that the island was a stone's cast from the town, 'upon which stands a castle, and at the foot of this mountain the ships cast anchor.' Tomé Pires, a Portuguese apothecary who was sent to India in 1511 as the factor-in-charge of drugs, travelled with a fleet of ships commanded by the nephew of Afonso d'Albuquerque and described Sira as a 'beautiful fortress with a captain in it always prepared, as he should be, because for the last ten years they have always been afraid of our armadas.'

In March 1513 Afonso d'Albuquerque, the Portuguese second Viceroy of India, with some 3,000 troops, attempted an assault on the fortifications. His nephew led a party of soldiers to the walls with scaling ladders, but the weight of the men on the ladders caused them to break. These dramatic accounts were recorded by local historians.

Aden's importance as an entrepot grew with the expansion of trade between India, China and the Mediterranean. Chau ja–kua, an inspector of foreign taxes in Fukien, used the accounts brought back by eye-witnesses. 'The king of the country, the officers and the

**Aden in the 1860s during the British occupation. The lone minaret in the centre is
possibly all that remains of a great mosque built by the Umayyad Caliph Umar bin Abdul
Aziz in the early part of the 8th century.**   *ILN*

people all worship Heaven. The gentry wear turbans of white silk falling down the back,
they have designs in gold thread in them. Their clothes are made of white yue-no stuff with
gold characters in it, or else of brocades of sundry kinds. They eat wheaten cakes, meat
and milk. The poor eat fish and vegetables. The soil does not produce rice.'

The trade in spices – the most important of all – was dominated by Cairene merchants
who built their storehouses in Crater, the main township of Aden, while the Egyptian fleet
kept all foreign shippers out of the Red Sea, causing them to load and offload their cargoes
in Aden. The transhipment charge on pepper alone amounted to a third of its value.

Circa 1508, di Varthema found the city of Aden 'extremely beautiful' with five castles on
the mountains, and estimated that there were some five or six thousand families. A hundred
years later the first English seafarers described the town as ruined, with few good houses
left standing. The position of Aden as a centre of trade between East and West, with ships
using the Red Sea route, was undermined when Vasco da Gama 'discovered' the sea route
from Portugal to India, and rounded the Cape of Good Hope in 1498. Added to this, coffee
from north Yemen had become popular in Europe and this brought prosperity to Mocha.
By 1608, it had replaced Aden as the most important trading centre in Yemen.

House and church of the Roman Catholic Mission built in Aden *circa* **1880s-90s.** *Massaja I.83*

In Aden the Turks left behind them newly built or repaired fortifications. The local historian and Qadhi, Abu Abdullah bin Ahmed Muhsin, considered that most of the fortifications were built in the twelfth century by Othman al-Zenjilly, appointed Governor of Aden by the Ayyubid, Turanshah, brother of Salah al-Din ibn Ayyub. Another reminder of the Turkish occupation was recorded by the Frenchman, Jean de la Roque, in his book *A Voyage to Arabia Felix*, published in 1716. He noted accounts made by French merchants during their voyages to Yemen in the years 1708-10: 'there are not to be seen of the kind, fairer stoves and baths than those of this town, they are all lin'd with marble or jasper, and cover'd with a fair dome, through which the light comes, which is adorned within side galleries, supported by magnificent columns.' In 1832 Lt James Wellsted, a surveyor on board the East India Company ship, *Palinurus*, commented: 'Of the spacious and commodious baths lined with jasper, not a vestige … now remains.' Just before the British occupation, Wellsted in 1835 wrote: 'All that remains of the former city are a few minarets, about a hundred houses', and Captain Stafford Bettesworth Haines of the Indian Navy, remarked that in 1838, 'the little village (formerly the great city) of Aden is now reduced to the most exigent condition of poverty and neglect.'

In January 1839 the British took Aden by force and occupied it for nearly 129 years. Haines was officially confirmed in his post as Political Agent in Aden in October 1839. Aden's natural crater they named Crater, which the Yemenis call Aden. Many of its streets were laid out in orderly lines by the British military men who planned them. In 1877 Captain F. M. Hunter, Assistant Resident Aden, noted that Aden consisted of about 2,000 whitewashed houses and was divided into streets and lanes. 'Many of the houses are double-storied but none are noteworthy for their architecture.'

It was from Sultan Muhsin bin Fadhl al-Abdali that the British had taken Aden. The Abdali Sultans had their capital at Al-Hauta. *Al-Hauta* is common in tribal areas as it signifies a sanctuary where tribal feuding is forbidden; it might be a market town where traders could carry on their business in peace, or it might be a shrine where pilgrimages take place. Al-Hauta, now the capital of Lahej Governorate, is commonly referred to as Lahej. It was always a large market centre where caravans assembled for their journeys north to the highlands or south to Aden. The name Lahej

Captain Stafford Bettesworth Haines, 1802-1860. (Courtesy of Michael Waterfield, from *Sultans of Aden* **by Gordon Waterfield.)**

denotes land which is low lying, intersected by water channels – a name which admirably describes the area. On the plain, watered by the River Tiban and richly fertile, exotic fruits, luxuriant foliage and wild flowering shrubs flourish. Some genealogists connect the name Lahej with a Himyarite called Lahj bin Wa'il.

Henry Salt took the opportunity to explore Lahej during his visit in the early 1800s. He was led to the Sultan's palace, where he had an audience with Sultan Ahmed bin Abd al-Karim al-Abdali, whom he described as 'an old man, of a very patriarchal appearance, with a benign yet intelligent expression in his countenance. He received us in a very friendly manner.' Salt had 'few observations to make' on the town of Lahej. 'The inhabitants manufacture a species of fine coloured striped cloths, peculiar to the country, which forms the common dress of Arabs of rank.

'To the north of the town flourished an extensive grove of date, mango, sycamore and pomegranate trees, among which I observed several lofty and fine trees, called by the Arabs bedan – the fruit – resembling an almond. The quantity of water required for cultivation in this place is astonishing; the soil round the trees is obliged to be kept constantly moist.' He speaks highly of the Sultan's manner of administering the affairs of the town and neighbouring districts and 'by his constant solicitude for the welfare of his subjects, has fully become entitled to the appellation of "Father of his country" which is now bestowed upon him by his people.'

Walter Harris visited Lahej at the end of the nineteenth century and had an audience with the then Sultan of Lahej, Fadhl bin Ali Muhsin al-Abdali. The traveller refers to him as 'a pleasant-spoken old gentleman, extremely fond of showing off various treasures he possesses.' Harris was invited to smoke from a water-pipe which he found was 'a sore trial ... However, so attentive was the Sultan in handing me the amber mouthpiece that I stuck bravely to the

Above: Aden is situated in a volcanic crater. After the British occupied Aden, it was given the name Crater. In the centre, stands a lone minaret, to the left is the 'former palace of the Abdali Sultan, at present [early 1850s] inhabited by the British Political Agent'. Bernatz estimated the population 'as 2100 souls'. To the right is the Aidrous mosque, and in the foreground a camel caravan nears the *aqaba* between Ma'alla and Crater.   *BernatzPl.II*

Left: The Mansuri range: 'In the centre of Cape Aden rises the lofty Jebel Shamsham [Shamsan]. It is about 1,800 feet high, overtopping all the other hills and mountains that surround it. The point chosen for taking the view here given is in a solitary valley separated from the Port of Aden by a row of basaltic hills.'   *BernatzPl.I*

The *aqaba* or main pass between Ma'alla and Crater drawn in the 1880s. *ILN*

Above: A tunnel between Aden (Crater) and the isthmus road was first cut in the tenth century. It was used through the centuries afterwards and gave easier access for water-bearing camels, or for that matter camels carrying any type of goods. *ILN*

Left: The Tawilah Reservoirs in the 1890s with garden and Aden (Crater) beyond. St Mary the Virgin sits on the lower slope in the centre. *Bizzoni 421*

Al-Hauta, known as Lahej, is the capital of the Lahej Governorate. The palace of the Abdali Sultan of Lahej is shown on the left.   *ILN*

task.' *Qat* or *catha edulis*, 'considered a necessary luxury', was also offered to him. The leaves of the plant are chewed and are said to 'cause a delightful state of wakefulness.'

On the way to the 'café', where he was staying, Harris visited the palace stables where there were a great many horses. He stated that there was 'little to see in Hauta', but thought that 'Perhaps the sights best worth noticing are in the market, where under the shade of an enormous *b'dam* tree sit women selling bread. ... Here also are exposed for sale vegetables, camel and horse fodder, and many other market products, which are sent on to Aden.' The bazaars: 'narrow covered-in streets with rough little mud-brick shops on either side, filled with cotton goods for the most of European manufacture; a few gaudy muslins from India ... giving a brilliant hue to some of these dusky little box-like shops. A whole bazaar is put aside for the workers in metals. It forms a thatched square, divided up by low walls, some three feet in height, like sheep pens, in which the various metal-workers sit, each with his forge. The scene is a most picturesque one. The sunlight falling in through holes in the ill-thatched roofing strikes upon the burnished metal until the daggers and spear-heads sparkle and glisten like diamonds. The air is hazy with the fumes of the forges, and rings with the never-ceasing fall of the hammer upon the metals.'

Al-Hauta 'lies in a great oasis, supplied with water from rivers flowing from the highlands.' It is richly cultivated. To the right is the mosque, with matted and thatched dwellings in front. 'The streets are narrow and built without any idea of regularity.. nor are the houses even built in any attempt at being in line .. Nearly all the houses are surrounded by these zarebas or yards, into which the cattle are driven of a night.' The Sultan's palace in early 1890 is in the background.   *Harris 60*

Adem

The view of 'Adem' as it appeared to Gaspar Correa at the time of the attack by the Portuguese in 1513, under Afonso d'Albuquerque. The turret-crested peaks of Jebel Shamsan loom behind the town and the fortified island of Sira is bottom left. Some 3,000 troops attempted an assault on the walls of Aden, which failed because 'the weight of the men climbing the ladders caused them to break'.   *FelnerII.342*

4
THE PEOPLE

Imam of the mosque of al-Mutawakkil, Sana'a, in the late
1870s wearing traditional costume.   *Manzoni 213*

Eighteenth & Nineteenth Century Personalities

Audience with Imam al-Mahdi Abbas bin al-Husayn bin al-Qasim of Sana'a. 'The audience took place in a large rectangular hall under an arched roof. In the middle was a fountain whose jets shot fourteen feet into the air. Behind the pool there was a raised platform, and behind this again another dais where the Imam's throne was situated. The entire floor both round the fountain and on the raised platforms was covered with Persian carpets. The throne itself consisted merely of a square dais covered with silks, on which had been placed three large cushions, one behind and one to each side of the Imam, all covered in very costly materials. The Imam himself sat on the throne among the cushions with his legs doubled beneath him in Oriental fashion. He was clad in a light green blouse with long wide sleeves. He had a large golden bow fastened to his cloak on both sides of his breast. On his right hand stood his sons, on his left his brothers. In front of him on the platform stood his Minister of State, Faqih Ahmed, and on the next step the expedition now took up its position. Along the walls as far as the door stood two long rows of Arab leaders.'

19 July 1763. 'We [Carsten Niebuhr and other members of the Danish expedition] were taken straight across to the Imam to kiss the back and palm of his right hand, and also his clothing where it hung down over one knee. The first and last of these are usual when one is received by Arab princes; but it is a mark of extraordinarily great honour if a foreigner is given the palm of the hand to kiss. Deep silence prevailed in the whole room. But the moment any of us touched the Imam's hand, a herald cried out certain words that apparently meant something like "Allah preserve the Imam". His cry was repeated by all those present, who seemed to shout the words with all the force of their lungs. As I went first and was thinking only of how to express my compliments in as good Arabic as possible and observing the magnificent splendour, the like of which I had not seen anywhere else in Arabia, I cannot deny that I was rather alarmed by this tremendous noise, especially as they began to shout at the very moment I touched the Imam's hand. I quickly recovered my composure, however, and as they began to shout again when my colleagues took the Imam's hand, it occurred to me that what was happening at this ceremony was rather like what happens at home when we call for three cheers.' *Niebuhr(2)I.Pl.LXI*

Qadhi, Imams and other dignitaries of Sana'a, late 1870s. *Manzoni 186*

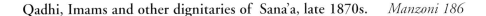

Castle of the Sultan of Lahej in the first decade of the nineteenth century. 'As we approached the town of Lahej, we were met by a deputation headed by the Dola of the place, who conducted us forwards, surrounded by his Ascari [soldiers], who marched on wildly, dancing, singing, tossing up their matchlocks, and shouting. This scene lasted until we reached the first entrance of the Sultan's house, when three irregular vollies of musquetry ended the ceremony. We were conducted thence through several passages, strongly barricaded at each end, up to an apartment opening to the sky ... on the far side of which Sultan Hamed was waiting to receive us. We found an old man, of a very patriarchal appearance, with a benign yet intelligent expression in his countenance. He received us in a very friendly manner, and seemed truly in his heart, as he repeated over and over again in the manner of the Arabians to feel great delight in once more beholding an Englishman before he died.'   *Salt 116*

Opposite: Audience with Sultan Ali Muhsin al-Abdali of Lahej, 1890s. Walter Harris sits to the left wearing a fez. 'The room in which the Sultan was seated was a large square chamber. A heavy beam of carved teak-wood ran down the centre of the ceiling, supported on pillars of the same material. The floor was richly carpeted in oriental rugs, and silk divans were arranged along the walls. Light was admitted by large windows, over the lower portion of

which was trellis work. At one corner of the room sat a group of men, some five or six in all; while on a table close by were three handsome silver hubble-bubble pipes from Hyderabad, tended and kept alight by a half-nude Arab in a blue loin-cloth.

'One of the group rose to meet me. He was a stout elderly man, with a kindly pleasing expression, dark in colour; and although not strictly handsome, he possessed a manner, common to most Orientals of position, that could not fail to charm. Grasping me by the hand, he led me to the divan where I seated myself beside him, and salutations over, proffered me the amber mouthpiece of his pipe and a bunch of *qat*.

'Sitting next to the Sultan was a Shereef, a descendant of the Prophet ... A gold dagger of great antiquity that he wore in his belt, and which he kindly showed to me, was as perfect a thing of its kind as it has ever been my lot to set eyes upon. The Sultan himself was robed in a long loose outer garment of dull olive green, displaying a kuftan beneath of yellow-and-white striped silk, fastened at the waist by a coloured sash. On his head he wore a large yellow silk turban, surrounded by a twisted cord of black camel's hair and gold thread. I had enjoyed my visit to the Sultan Ali, whom I found to be a pleasant-spoken kindly old gentleman ... During my visit I had been watched with great interest by two of the Sultan's children, a little boy and girl ... the boy nude except for his loin-cloth of striped silk, the girl dressed in a mauve garment embroidered in gold.' *Harris 170*

Ahmed bin Ali al-Abdali brother of Sultan Fadhl bin Ali al-Abdali of Lahej in the 1870s, wearing ceremonial dress. *Manzoni 11*

A Sayyid astride a prancing horse on the outskirts of Mocha. *GrandpréII.157*

During al-Mahdi Abbas's time, following the Friday Prayer, the Imam's or Dola's mounted escort performed exercises in the *maydan*, or square, before the Dola's palace. Niebuhr gives the following key to the figures:

'(1) The Dola's palace. (2) The citadel. (3) The mosque. (4) A common house. (5) the Dola, a sabre and shield to one side, a large turban on his head, the end of which falls between his shoulders, rides his horse, its

back covered with a polished steel blanket. (6) Mountain Arabs with their long hair bound into cloth. (7) The Commanding Officer with a small stick in his right hand. (8) Servants of the Dola wear a large turban, wide rolled-up shirts over a loincloth. (9) Well-to-do men. (10) Traditional dress of the Tihamah. (11) Mountain soldiers. (12) A camel, led by a cameleer, carries water pots. (13) Banyans, Hindu traders. (14) Clothing of the Jews. (15) Three of the Danish Expedition wearing Turkish dress.'
Niebuhr(I)Pl.XVI

Clothing and Headdresses

Costumes from Hadhramaut as described to L.W.C.van den Berg by Hadhramis living in the Dutch East Indies, 1890s.

Inhabitants of the towns, Sayyids, merchants, shopkeepers and so on varied more in their dress than did the tribesmen and bedouins. The *futah,* loincloth, was generally worn longer than the tribesman's and made from locally woven cotton cloth or imported brightly coloured silk sarongs from the East Indies. A popular dress for townsmen in Hadhramaut was the long white buttoned-up *qamis,* worn over the shirt and *futah.* A short coat was worn over it. Out of doors the Sayyids wore long cream-coloured coats, open in front, high hard caps, *kufiyya,* heavily embroidered with gold thread by the women and around it a turban. It is considered 'extremely negligent to go out bare-headed.' Although it is omitted from the illustrations, van den Berg wrote, 'they carry always on the shoulders a shawl, two and a half metres in length.' *Berg end*

The tribesmen wear a coloured *futah,* often locally woven, and a shirt which buttons up to a high-necked collar. A piece of brightly coloured cloth is twisted round the leather belt that holds up the *futah,* and in which the man carried his dagger, powder horn and other paraphernalia and often holds a matchlock. They wear turbans of bright colours over crocheted skull caps. In the past, one would tell from which area the man came by the way in which he tied his turban.   *Berg end*

The women's dresses are wide with sleeves and large shoulders, the neck cut as a square. The dresses are cut just above the ankles in the front but have a short train at the back. 'On going outside they put on their wide trousers, which are gathered at the ankles ... the women's hairstyle was tiny plaits ... the women cover their head with a scarf or veil ... and cover their body in a very wide coat.' The borders of the dresses are embroidered with silver sometimes. They wear jewellery and have pierced ears and wear a number of earrings in each ear: 'fifteen or even more ... For shoes the Hadhrami women wore sandals, but also *les bottines* red or yellow; the Beduin women went barefoot.' *Berg end*

Left: Al-Gheidha, Mahra in 1836. 'The Sheikh was dressed in every respect except the turban which bore a strong likeness to the headdress of Jupiter Ammon, the turban cloth lying twisted up in such a manner as to look like the Cornu Ammonia seen on some of the coins of Alexander the Great, his *soi-disant* son; and by way of distinction a round pillow was always placed for him to sit upon.' *NicholsonPl.V*

Right: Al-Gheidha, Mahra. The Shaykh's son in 1836. 'The men, particularly the younger ones, (a few of the older wearing turbans) each having a long blue mantle hanging about him precisely as some of the ancients are represented with a long fringe of strings descending from all its edges. A straight single edged sword with a hook or deep notch near the end of the hilt, and a cross piece between that and the blade ... some of them carry a very primitive spear, and always a dagger or creese very much crooked – and usually in a silver sheath – some of them had shields covered with leather, with three or four large embossed knobs or bosses of brass or silver on them; the shield being about one foot in diameter – But the headdress formed the most curious part of their attire; consisting of a bushy head of hair of considerable length standing quite upright (most likely stiffened in that position by gum) with gaudy red and yellow handkerchief bound round the forehead.' *NicholsonPl.II*

75

Left: A tribesman, from the south, wearing an indigo-dyed loincloth and holding a matchlock rifle. He has a dagger in his waistband with a powder horn and tobacco box attached. *Schweinfurth 609*

Sometimes a tribesman went barefoot, although he usually possessed home-made sandals which had overhanging straps that flapped as he walked and which were said to frighten away snakes and scorpions. He wore a silver armlet set with cornelians, silver rings, and a cornelian amulet set in silver and strung on a thread round his neck. Another popular charm was a piece of dark cotton twisted round the leg below the knees to give strength to his limbs.

Above: Fadhli tribesmen. The elder, on horseback, holds a sword in his right hand and his companions carry matchlocks.   *Schweinfurth 605*

Below: **A bedouin holding a basket of produce, near Hodeidah.** *NicholsonPl.XII*

Above: **The chief of the Beni al-Harith tribe of central Yemen stands with his son.** *Manzoni 44*

Below: **A bedouin smoking a long wooden pipe, near Qunfidah**. *NicholsonPl.XVI*

Right: **A father and son from the north, dressed in rich bedouin costume.** *Manzoni 24*

Above: Imaginative portrayal of costumes worn in Socotra. According to Arnold von Harff's description in 1496: 'in Schoyra [Socotra] are good Christians of St.Thomas's beliefs. They are for the most part rich, but there are also poor people. They pray devoutly and long in their churches. They all wear long dyed linen cloaks and bind round their heads – men and women – blue turbans, and all go barefoot.' *Groote 138*

Above: A Somali man (left) and the son of the Dola of Musa, Tihamah (right). Lord Valentia wrote that Mr. Salt 'drew the town of Musa and also the Dola's son who did the honours of the place, his father being absent.' *Annesley 276*

Right: A young boy from Mocha in his holiday clothes, 1800s. 'Great rejoicings were made on account of the accession of the new sovereign ... during this day and the three following, there was a continual firing of cannon and musquetry, with other tokens of festivity. The inhabitants were all dressed out in their holiday clothes, and a gaiety spread itself through the town.' *Salt 300*

Above left: Profile of a man wearing a turban over his 'raven-black locks'. *Harris 78*

Above right: A Yemeni Jew wearing a skull cap. In the 1890s Walter Harris estimated the number of Jews in Sana'a to be 20,000. They had a quarter to themselves and 'are free to carry on whatever trade they will; to attend their synagogues and schools ... they pay their regular share in taxation.' *Harris 82*

Right: A man from the Tihamah, clutching a spear in his left hand, his 'long glossy locks tumbling in unrestrained glory over the shoulders, girded with his loin-cloth of dark blue cotton' and dagger fixed into his waist cloth, with silver armlet.   *Harris 68*

Above left: **An Indian Muslim from Aden.**
Manzoni 244

Above right: **An employee in the Italian consulate, Aden.** *Manzoni 2*

Right: Banyan, Hindu trader, from Aden.
Manzoni 259

Right: **A Parsee from Aden.**
Manzoni 258

Left: **A Mahratti from Aden.** *Manzoni 257*

Above: **A young girl from Jelileh, north of Dhala.** *Harris 204*

Above: **A man and woman of the highlands.** 'The men wear their hair long ... they wear a thick sheep-skin coat, the wool on the inside. The women wear dark blue skirts, embroidered round the neck and sleeves and on the breasts in coloured silks and now and again on gold and silver thread. Their heads they cover with dark-blue hoods, often richly but coarsely embroidered.' *Harris 228*

Right: **A girl carrying pots, dressed in trousers and dress embroidered at neck, knees and ankles.** In Wadi Khoreiba, '... great, bare rocky mountains rose on either side .. the valley itself was green and fresh, birds chirruped, great painted butterflies sailed by, monkeys and apes chattered and grunted on the steep mountain-sides.' *Harris 198*

Left: Cartsten Niebuhr related: 'We passed the night at Bulgosa. Several of the men of the village came to see us; and, after they retired, we had a visit from our hostess, with some young women accompanying her, who were all very desirous to see the Europeans ... their faces were unveiled; and they talked freely with us ... Mr. Baurenfeind drew a portrait of a young girl who was going to draw water, and was dressed in a shirt of linen, chequered blue and white. The top and middle of the shirt, as well as the lower part of her drawers, were embroidered with needle-work of different colours.' Above her right ear tucked into her scarf is a sweet-scented herb. *Niebuhr(2)I.Pl.LXIV*

Right: A woman at Luhayyah. '...though very retired, whether married or unmarried, they are not less careful of their dress and persons. At home they wear nothing but a long shift of fine cotton-cloth, suitable to their quality. They dye their feet and hands with henna, not only for ornament, but as an astringent, to keep them dry from sweat. They wear their own hair, which is plaited, and falls in long tails behind.' *BruceI.308*

A woman from the Tihamah with painted markings on her face. *Niebuhr(2)I.Pl.LIX*

Above: A *mafraj*, or reception room, 'carpeted with rugs and striped cloths. A number of handsome bronze brasiers and strange bowls and coffee pots. Sunk into the walls were alcoves, in which scent-bottles and sprinklers, cups and saucers ... were standing. The effect of the light falling through [the alabaster windows] ... was soft and luxurious, a rosy yellow in colour.' A man attends to the charcoal for the hubble-bubble.   *Harris 260*

Below: A woman from Ta'izz smoking a traditional water-pipe.   *Manzoni 9*

Left: A woman from al-Hauta, Lahej.
Manzoni 13

Opposite: 'The whole dress of the Arabs is admirably adapted to the climate.' Mocha can be seen in the background.
GrandpréII.174

Below left: A Sanani girl enveloped in a black cloak. The *usbah*, headband, headdress, can be quite an elaborate affair. A typical *usbah*, in order of placing the articles on the head, includes: a plain dark headscarf; a narrow dark cloth, held together by piercing long pins, ending in silver or other ornamentation, through it, often it is wound under the chin and over the head; a single piece of satin or silk worked heavily with gold or silver thread and with sequins or coins.
Manzoni 387

Below: An assortment of footwear.
Niebuhr(1)Pl.II

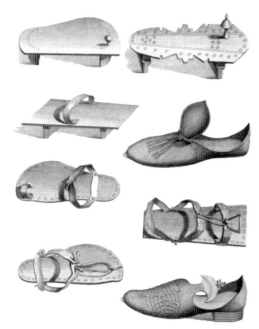

Trade and the Market Place

Above: 'On we walked between the high walls of gardens, out onto the street, to where, in its little grove of palm-trees, stands the tomb of the patron saint, Sheik Othman, with its domes and its mosque and strange tower of sun-dried bricks.' Shaykh Othman, 'now a flourishing township', was famed for its indigo-dyeing. Cameleers, with long spears, organise business deals before rejoining the caravan-roads laden with cargo for different destinations. 'The camels of the southern district of the Yemen are famous for their breed and fleetness. They are slightly built, with fine legs.' *Harris 122*

Right: A *khan* near Yarim. 'Farther in [the *khan*] the space served as a stable, and there were quite a number of camels, mules and donkeys within its precincts ... a staircase leading up to a long gallery. The buttresses supporting the roof divided the gallery into compartments and it seemed to be the custom for a party ... to spread their carpets and smoke their hubble-bubbles, calling to the khan servants below for their coffee and food and charcoal for their pipes.' *Harris 248*

Above: Tribesmen from Central Yemen selling produce.   *Manzoni 47*

Above: Musicians from Fadhli territory in the south: a woman with tambourine on the left and on her left a man playing a *mizmar*, or short flute.   *Manzoni 19*

Below: A group of cameleers.   *Manzoni 67*

Below: A mountain woman carrying firewood in the Sana'a suq.   *Manzoni 79*

The south quarter of the Red Sea port of Mocha. Outside the walls can be seen boat building to the right and packaged goods being loaded and unloaded.   *Annesley II.347*

The bazaar at Dhamar. 'Although at times a considerable crowd thronged us, we found the people extremely polite, and what little inconvenience we were put to was owing entirely to the curiosity of the inhabitants. The bazaars boast little beyond their natural picturesqueness.' Canopies shade the 'one-storeyed box-like dens' and the trades are divided up into separate streets and quarters. *Harris Frontispiece*

Above: **An Adeni Jew selling ostrich feathers (left) and a money changer (right) in Aden.** *MassajaVIII.113.*

Left: **A banyan, or Hindu trader of al-Gheidha, Mahra.** 'The banyans were dressed something like their conquerors of India but differed in the turban which was large and flat on the head.' *NicholsonPl.IX*

The bazaar at Hodeidah in 1836 with a man smoking a water-pipe. Household goods, guns, daggers and different produce in baskets are displayed.   *NicholsonPl.XIV*

Above: The lowest cistern at Tawilah Reservoirs, Aden, with a small orchard behind. In front men with their camels collect water.   *Manzoni 310*

Below: The camel park and fodder market in Aden in the 1870s, with the Christian cemetery behind.   *Manzoni 292*

Agriculture and Pastoral Life

'Bulgosa, one of those villages whose inhabitants subsist upon the profits which their crops of coffee afford. Neither asses nor mules can be used here: the hills are to be climbed by narrow and steep paths ... the scenery seemed to me charming; as it was covered with gardens and plantations of coffee-trees.

'The coffee-trees were all in flower in Bulgosa, and exhaled an exquisitely agreeable perfume. They are planted upon terraces, in the form of an amphitheatre. Most of them are watered by the rains that fall. Stones being more common in this part of the country ... the houses ... are built of this material ... they have a good appearance; especially such of them as stand upon the heights, with beautiful gardens, and trees.' *Niebuhr(2)I.Pl.LXIII*

'I soon came within sight of the small town of Hadie [west of Bayt al-Faqih] ... a place well
known to Europeans; who come hither from Beit el Fakih, to pass some time occasionally in
this little town, where the air is cool, and the water fresh and pure. It is, however, but ill-built,
and has nothing else of consequence, except its trade in coffee, which the inhabitants of the
hills bring down upon certain days in the week. After the duties are paid to the Dola, the
coffee is packed up and conveyed upon camels, either to Beit el Fakih or directly to Hodeidah.
We enjoyed a singular and beautiful prospect from the house of the Sub-Dola at Hadie.'
Niebuhr(2)I.Pl.LXV

Below (from left): **A pottery vessel to hold** *qishr* – a hot drink made from grilled coffee husks boiled in water with ginger added. The fibres at the top of the *gebana*, or coffee pot, act as a strainer when *qishr* is poured. The coffee bean was usually exported. To the right a silver coffee cup holder and a pottery coffee cup; and a rosewater sprinkler to the far right. *Niebuhr(1)Pl.I*

Right: Coffee terraces in Attara, near Manakha. 'From an expanse of terraced slope rises a single pinnacle of rock some hundreds of feet in height. On the very summit is a large building ... there is a stairway cut in the solid rock, by means of which the inhabitants ascend and descend ... nestling under the pinnacle is the rest of the village, built tier above tier on the steep mountain-side.' *Harris 8*

Right: A view taken from Wa'alan's terraces south of Sana'a. *Harris 288*

Agricultural paraphernalia:

A: Ploughing with oxen.
B: Drawing water from a well, sometimes donkeys or oxen are used.

C: Wooden plough.
D: A large stone object, which is dragged over wheat to crush it.
E: Sawing wood.

F: Because there are so few trees in the Tihamah, farmers erect scaffolding to provide shade and to act as a lookout tower.
G: Using a pickaxe to dig the ground.
H: Two men use a long spade-like blade to dig a small canal for water to flow through gardens and fields.
Niebuhr(1)Pl.XV

Left: A pastoral hut with a rounded grass roof, in the Tihamah. *Niebuhr(I)Pl.I*

99

Above: **A uniformed British officer (foreground) surveys the pastoral scene of Socotra, with rock cave dwellers in the distance.** *Wellsted(2)II.Frontispiece*

Below: 'The people [of Socotra] are entirely pastoral.' Henry Forbes and his party found 'luxuriant ankle-deep sward of succulent herbage on which grazed sheep and goats and large herds of the extremely beautiful dwarf cattle.' The cattle 'belong to a very small, shorthorned, deep dewlapped, unhumped breed, differing entirely from those of the lands nearest to Socotra.' *Forbes xliv*

Dracaena cinnabari. **Two types of Dragon's Blood trees on Socotra. The men have made incisions into the bark in order to obtain the blood-red resin, seen oozing from the trunks.** *BalfourPl.XCVI*

Socotri pottery fashioned by women and decorated with the red resin of the Dragon's Blood tree. *Forbes frontispiece*

Above: Three pots used to contain milk, ghee or aloe juices. The two on the right would be used particularly for cooking or for heating milk.

Above: Pots used as water vessels; the pot top left would have contained water for religious ablutions.

Below: Two pottery bowls used for food.

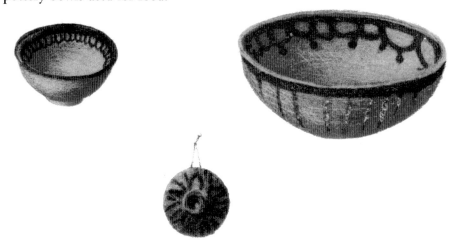

Above: Small pot hung on the wall for ornamental purposes when not in use for burning incense. Most of the dwellings had earth floors so that utensils could be pressed into the ground to make them stand upright.

5

HADHRAMAUT

Shihr in 1894. An old minaret towers above its mosque.
Graphic

Known to earliest antiquity, the name Hadhramaut occurs in Genesis in its Hebrew form, Hazarmaveth, and the Greek and Roman authors spoke of the people of the Atramitae and the Chatramotitae; the country they called Hadramyta. Qabr Hud – considered the most holy spot in Hadhramaut – is the tomb of the Prophet Hud who is thought to be the patriarch Eber in Genesis. This unique civilisation was scarcely known to the West before the beginning of the nineteenth century.

Shihr, the coastal region, was the name given to the whole coast extending from west of the port of Shihr to Dhofar, now in the Sultanate of Oman, to the east. The port of Shihr was, for many centuries, the gateway to the towns and villages of Wadi Hadhramaut and other inland settlements. According to Al-Masudi it was also an important market town for the Mahri from the region of Mahra, east of Hadhramaut, to whom it once belonged. Ali bin Husayn, a native of Baghdad, was called al-Mas'udi after one of the Prophet's companions, Abdullah bin Mas'ud to whom he traced his descent. The fourteenth century scholar, ibn Khaldun, called Mas'udi the 'Imam of all historians'. He was also known as the 'Herodotus of the Arabs'. From Shihr many emigrants from the interior and from the coastal districts sailed to the East Indies or to East Africa to seek their fortunes. The Dutchman, L.W.C. van den Berg, in his masterly book, *Le Hadhramaut et les Colonies Arabes dans l'Archipel Indien*, 1886, wrote that the women refused to 'follow their husbands outside their country'. Van den Berg never visited Yemen, but compiled a remarkable survey and carried out his detailed researches on Hadhramaut among the Arabs in the Dutch East Indies, 'who nearly all originated from Hadhramaut'.

'A great deal of white incense grows in this country', wrote the thirteenth century Venetian explorer, Marco Polo, 'and brings in a great revenue to the Prince, for no one dares sell it to anyone else ... Dates also grow very abundantly here ... The natives live on meat and rice and fish.' He called the coast 'Esher', adding that it had a king who was subject to the 'Soldan of

The north gate of Shihr in 1894. For many centuries, Shihr was the gateway to the towns and villages of Wadi Hadhramaut and other inland settlements. *Graphic*

Aden'. Three hundred years later the Portuguese adventurer, Duarte Barbosa, called it 'Xaer' and found it to be a large place with a 'great store of goods from many kinds of merchandise' and the harbour a 'great resort for numbers of ships'. The Portuguese adventurers, however, were no more welcome in Shihr than they had been in Aden. A local historian recorded: 'On Thursday 929 [1512-13] the abandoned Frank, may God abandon him, came to the port of al-Shihr with about nine sailing ships ... and, landing in the town on Friday, set to fighting a little after dawn. Not one of the people was able to withstand him: on the contrary they were horribly routed, and the Lord of the town ... God rest him, died for the faith ... The town was shamefully plundered, the Franks looting it first, then after them the musketeers, and the soldiers, and the hooligans of the town in consequence of which people were reduced to poverty.'

Admiral Pieter van Broecke of the Dutch East India Company tried unsuccessfully to start a factory at Aden in 1614, but he had better fortune at Shihr, where he was allowed to open one. He described the town of Shihr: 'situated on a dry sandy beach in a large bay where one can have good anchor ... The town seems large because the houses are so far from each other, they are all made of mud with chalk covered walls. There is a castle with four round towers ... There are three or four mosques. This is the principal port of the King.'

Lt Wellsted in the 1830s was surprised to find no coffee houses in Shihr, 'so numerous in other parts of Arabia', but by careful enquiry found it was customary to drink in each other's houses, 'it being indecorous to be seen doing so in public.'

The Shihri coast was, and is, teeming with fish. Marco Polo observed 'that all their cattle, including horses, oxen and camels live upon small fish and nought besides.' For years dried shark, a source of protein, was loaded onto camels' backs to be eaten up-country as a necessary part of the diet of caravaneers and travellers alike.

Little mention is made of Mukalla, to the west of Shihr, in the records of very early travellers because Shihr was then of far greater importance, but by the time Wellsted came

The Jemadar's house near the sea at Shihr. Above the carved wooden screens are ventilation apertures. Rooms on the upper floors open out on to terraces which are surrounded by a high wall with tracery at the top. These terraces provide privacy and are also used for sleeping in the summer. *Graphic*

along in 1834 it had become a sizeable port. 'From seaward the houses have a lofty castellated appearance, the lower portion being constructed of stone, and the upper of sunburnt bricks ... The windows are small, and mostly facing the sea ... Glass is not used ... Loopholes for musketry occur at every storey.' Ventilation apertures usually 'occur at every storey' and are placed close to the ceiling above each window, as depicted in the drawings of houses in Mukalla.

With no room to expand the overflow population of Mukalla, the place where ships take refuge, spread out west to the camel park at Therb, across the river to Sherij, where many of the Subians live and are said to be descended from early Abyssinians, to Dis inland, and to Khalf in the east. On the headland, Ras Mukalla, stood, 'The white palace of the Sultan, which is six storeys high, with little carved windows and a pretty sort of cornice of open-work bricks', as noted by the first British woman traveller to Hadhramaut, Mabel Bent, at the end of the nineteenth century. From its windows could be seen the tomb of Sheikh Ya'qub Yusuf, the Patron Saint of Mukalla, who came from Baghdad in the thirteenth century, when Mukalla was a fishing village. The town itself presented a remarkably attractive picture – in front, the sea, and Qarat al-Mukalla, the limestone cliffs behind the town, rising to a height of some 1,300 feet. Mukalla's importance grew as a gateway to Shibam, in Wadi Hadhramaut, and other inland towns, gradually taking over from Shihr which, however, remained for several hundred years the gateway to Seiyun and Tarim in the Hadhramaut valley.

Between the 1850s and 1880s, slaves from East Africa were collected and placed in the slave depôts of Shihr and Mukalla, and then distributed to different parts of Arabia.

Opposite: Ras Mukalla, the headland of Mukalla, also known as al-Bilad, 1890s: '... we climbed on an undulating plateau about 600 feet above the sea ... on the edge of this plateau are a line of watch towers with some small attempts at a loopholed wall – these are intended to prevent the incursions of enemies from the landside, and were used in a recent war [Battle of Baqrain]. This plateau is composed principally of limestone of the same nature of the cliffs - and covered with loose pieces. There are a few small fields where jowaree is said to be grown during the rains. The views from the summit of Jebel al-Karate [Qarat al-Mukalla, where this drawing was made] was very fine, the sea being so clear that the bottom was distinctly visible and, where sandy, the shadows of the boats in the bottom.' To the right of the cemetery with the tomb of Sheikh Ya'qub, is the mosque of al-Rodha on the waterfront.   *Molesworth*

Below: Mukalla: the Jemadar's palace and harbour, 1890s. 'We remained in as the Sultan's son Ghalib was expected, about 8 a.m. He arrived with about 150 Arabs as an escort, the Jemadar and Vizier went out to meet him and escorted him in ... He went to the Jemadar's palace ... we came ashore at 3.30 and went to Ghalib bin Awad at the Jemadar's palace. I had met him before in Hyderabad. He was very cordial and asked if we wanted anything.'   *Molesworth*

Agreements were entered into between Mukalla and the British Political Resident Aden 'to abolish and prohibit the export, or import of slaves.'

Some three hundred miles northward of Mukalla, across stony plateaux which seem to stretch to eternity and are cut by a tangled web of valleys, lies the legendary Wadi Hadhramaut between majestic cliffs rising to well over 1,000 feet, the walls of which resemble magnificent ramparts. To the east of Tarim it continues as Wadi Masilah, the 'Valley of Floods', to Seihut on the coast of Mahra. Deep narrow ravines flow into the broad Wadi Hadhramaut – the most famous, Wadi Do'an, is identified with Pliny's 'Thoani' and is possibly the 'Thebane' of Ptolemy. Nine hundred feet below the perpendicular cliffs of the valley runs a river of dark green date palms mingled with the lighter green of 'elb trees and cultivation. In the past, out of the pale brown sand-coloured cliffs appeared great houses, so harmonising with their backgrounds as to be almost invisible; Do'an is one of the ancient routes to Wadi Hadhramaut. Nowadays some owners paint their houses in bright colours. Graffiti on rocks and stones by the wayside are believed to date from the first century BC to the early centuries AD, and consist mainly of proper names, often accompanied by drawings and symbols. The Bavarian, Baron von Wrede, travelled across the immense plateau until, 'The sudden appearance of the Wadi Do'an took me by surprise and impressed me much with the grandeur of the scene ... The road that leads down into the Wadi is a very dangerous one.' At Khoreiba, von Wrede was received 'with all possible hospitality by Sheikh Abdullah Ba Sudan, a man celebrated for the influence he has in the country and for the reputation of sanctity he has attained.'

'Stop, let us weep on account of the remembrances of my beloved and her abode on the edge of the sandy desert.' Hadhramaut's renowned pre-Islamic poet, Imru al-Qais of the princely tribe of Kinda, is said to have visited Wadi Do'an. In his most famous poem he remembers his beloved and his homeland. This was one of the poems of the *Mu'allaqat*, the 'Suspended Poems', so called because they were hung on the Ka'aba on account of their merit at the fair of Ukaz near Mecca, where pre-Islamic poets met in competition to recite their verses.

Hadhramaut has long been known as one of the greatest centres of learning in the Islamic world. In Seiyun and Tarim, religious academies drew students from many parts of the world, and contribution for their support came from many places, as far as India and Indonesia. Although Hadhramaut was geographically isolated, it became known also through its young men leaving their valley to earn a livelihood abroad to support their families, many to the East Indies or East Africa. The Sayyid writers affirm that the great migrations to Africa took place in the fourteenth and fifteenth centuries. Many learned men of Seiyun and Tarim are Sayyids, descendants of the Prophet Mohammed, who are said to have a common ancestor, Ahmed bin Isa, known as al-Muhajir, 'the Emigrant'. After leaving Basra in the tenth century he lived for a short while in Hajarein and then settled in Wadi Hadhramaut. As a descendant of Fatima, daughter of the Prophet Mohammed, he was much revered. His tomb, painted white, stands out on the hillside on the road from Seiyun to Tarim.

Wadi Hadhramaut, two to four miles wide, runs parallel to the south coast. Its wells and controlled flash floods provided much-needed water for cultivation and its rich soil yielded three or four crops a year where irrigation was successfully managed. This cultivation, gave the economic basis for a city-dwelling people, who built and inhabited the towering mud brick buildings of the towns of which the chief were Al-Qatn, Shibam, Seiyun and Tarim.

The imposing palace of the Kathiri Sultans in their capital city of Seiyun is also built of mud-brick mixed with straw, and dominates the town. It is now an important museum and research centre. On the lower floors were reception rooms for the Sultan and his guests; the ladies of the household lived on the top floors. Large numbers of Kathiri emigrated to Java where they made their fortunes enabling them to send revenue to help their families.

Above: Mukalla with Qarat al-Mukalla behind topped with turrets for defence purposes. *Schweinfurth 613*

Below: Mukalla in the 1890s, with moored dhows and the imposing palace of the Jemadar behind. *Graphic*

Above: **Mukalla: the place where ships take refuge.** *Molesworth*

'After Tarim you desire nothing more,' is a Hadhrami saying, and in the days when the town was isolated from the turmoil of the outside world, it must have seemed an oasis of tranquillity. Tarim's long history is said to date from the fourth century AD. It was the capital of the tribe of Kinda and is named after its king, Tarim bin Hadhramaut bin Saba al-Asghar. Tarim's master masons earned a well-deserved countrywide reputation for their skill in utilising local resources, and producing masterpieces of colourful decoration out of a foundation of mud. The extraordinary adaptability of this medium for building is to be seen throughout the wadi.

Mabel and Theodore Bent visited Qu'aiti territory in 1893/4. In a report to the Government of Bombay, the Political Resident Aden wrote on 18 August 1901, that the Bents were 'well received' by the Qu'aiti family: 'At that time, Ghalib, son of the Jemadar, was Governor of Mukalla. Shibam and its dependencies were under another nephew of the Jemadar, Salah, son of Mohammed. Hussein was at Shihr and apparently exercised some sort of general control over the others.'

Mr and Mrs Bent stayed for several days at Al-Qatn palace as guests of the Sultan. 'Like a fairy palace of the Arabian Nights, white as a wedding cake, and with as many battlements and pinnacles, with its windows painted red, the colour being made from the red sandstone, and its balustrades decorated with the inevitable chevron pattern, the castle of Al Koton [Al-Qatn] rears its battlemented towers above the neighbouring brown houses and expanse of palm groves.' They received a warm welcome: 'at his gate stood Sultan Salah to greet us, clad in a long robe of canary-coloured silk, and with a white silk turban twisted around his swarthy brow. He was a large, stout man, negroid in type, for his mother was a slave, and as generous as he was large, to Arab and European alike.' Of the interior of the palace Mabel Bent wrote: 'One of the most striking features of these Arabian palaces is the wood-carving. The doors are exquisitely decorated with it, the supporting beams, and the windows, which are adorned with fretwork instead of glass.'

Left: **Baqrain, with the castellated forts of 'Guful and Ghazi' sitting astride the route. '... [we] went up as far as a village called Bakrain – the river bed is about 300 yards wide and bricks are made from ... loam which has been deposited about three feet below the surface. Salt pans are also worked in the river bed.'** *Molesworth*

[The artist painted Baqrain as a panorama – a scene too broad for one canvas, thus causing a break in the view.]

'... arrived at Harshyat [1890s], which is a very small village with a few palm trees in the valley and some watch towers round it on low hills. The sea is visible from the low hills ... it was quite dark when we got in and Ghalib was most kind and showed us our rooms, which were the best in the village, before he went to his own lodging, which was not nearly as good.'
Molesworth

'Tabale is built on the top of a low gently rising hill, on the very summit there is a large house and apparently under this house is a hot water spring. Sulphorous gases escape with the hot water, but not in any large quantity. The water when it first comes out must be nearly boiling, when cooled it is very fair drinking water. It waters the hill in all directions and there is quite a grove of date trees and some tobacco is grown.'   *Molesworth*

Above: Water from a well is fed into a *siqaya*, a small reservoir containing drinkable water for travellers. The *siqaya* was usually constructed with money from a *waqf*, an endowment left by some charitably-minded person. The endowment also included money to pay for someone to ensure that the *siqaya* was kept filled with water. This image was drawn from descriptions given by Hadhramis living in the Dutch East Indies.   *Berg end*

Below: Al-Ghurfa, with the valley cliffs in the background. 'The principal towns to the east of Shibam are: al-Ghurfah, Saioun (the most important town), Taribah, al-Ghoraf, as-Sowairi, Terim (the ancient capital, but today surpassed by Saioun), 'Inat and al-Qasm. It was quoted in a newspaper ... that al-Ghurfah had 3000 people, but my informants quoted 1,500.' Drawn from descriptions given by Hadhramis living in the Dutch East Indies.   *Berg end*

Above: 'Castles of Hadhramaut.' Over a foundation of stone, the walls are made from mud and straw bricks dried by the sun. 'The buildings are fortified at each corner.' Elaborately carved window screens and doors are made from the local *'elb trees, zizyphus spina christi*. Drawn from descriptions given by Hadhramis living in the Dutch East Indies.   *Berg end*

Below: 'On nearing Ghail we were joined by about 60 matchlock men and for the last mile we advanced with the matchlock men firing into the air. Just by the walls of Ghail about 60 more matchlock men were drawn up who received us with a warm fusilade of blank, which was replied by our own escort until the two bodies joined when we moved on into the city.'   *Molesworth*

While Sultan Salah was arranging for the Bents' onward journey through the Kathiri towns of Seiyun and Tarim, and beyond to the tomb of the Prophet Hud in Wadi Masilah, Mabel Bent paid a visit to the ladies of Al-Qatn palace. 'Their examination of me was very searching', and while enjoying 'very good coffee with ginger and cloves in it', she 'did not feel very comfortable' when there was 'religious conversation and argument.'

The island town of Shibam, named after its king Shibam bin al-Harith bin Hadhramaut, must have been a phenomenal sight, as it still is today, to travellers who marvelled at its high buildings. A poet called it 'the sublime city', adding: 'Thou art the city of Hadhramaut.' Ibn Khaldun referred to Shibam as the largest city of Hadhramaut, in which 'the horses of the king are kept.' It has always been an important trading centre. Its merchants exported textiles and dates through the port of Shihr long before Islam came to the country. Mabel Bent remarked on the several industries carried on outside the walls, the chief one being the manufacture of indigo dye. She mentioned women of Wadi Do'an, wearing deep blue cotton dresses, 'decorated with fine embroidery and patches of yellow and red sewn on in patterns', being high in the front 'showing their yellow painted legs', and long at the back, just as they were described to van den Berg by Hadhramis living in the East Indies. The 'tall tapering hat' worn by the women can still be seen today in Wadi Hadhramaut.

Mr and Mrs Bent were fortunate to visit the tomb of the Prophet Saleh, north west of Shibam in Wadi Khonab, but did not visit the tomb of the Prophet Hud. The Prophet Saleh is believed to be the father of the Prophet Hud, who is also generally thought to be the patriarch named Eber in Genesis. Legend has it that Hud was pursued by two infidel horsemen. He disappeared into a cleft in the mountain that never completely closed behind him. His she-camel, which he couched outside the cleft, was turned to stone. A huge boulder near a many-columned cloister is said to be the hump of Hud's faithful camel. The town of Qabr Hud is only inhabited for three days in the year (although a few people come during the year to maintain their houses), when during the month of Sha'ban pilgrims visit his tomb – a place of tranquility.

6

THE TIHAMAH

Street scene in Hodeidah during the Turkish occupation, showing the Turkish Governor's office on the left, flying the Turkish flag.
Harris 189

The Tihamah – the semi-arid coastal plain of Yemen – stretches out along the Red Sea, which is itself an extension of the Rift Valley system of Africa. Contacts with Africa, separated only by a narrow lake or sea, have been close since the beginning of time. Ethiopian rulers acquired territory on the Tihamah at the start of the second century AD, and by the end of the same century had reached as far as Najran. For the next four centuries, Ethiopia remained an important player in the politics of the area. There are numerous descendants of slaves imported during Ethiopian rule in the sixth century. Whole populations were transported across the Red Sea to inhabit new towns in the Tihamah throughout the medieval period. Ethiopian words have crept into the Tihamah dialect. Circular huts with conical roofs are another similarity with Africa, and many species of trees and plants grow on each side of the Red Sea.

The Red Sea port of Mocha, which gave its name to the coffee grown in the highlands beyond.   *Dapper 30*

In the early ninth century, Zabid, a university town of great renown and a centre of culture and learning, was built by Mohammed ibn Ziyad. He traced his roots back to the Umayyad family and founded the Ziyadid dynasty in the tenth century. The Ziyadids ruled all the Tihamah and much of the highlands. The fourteenth century Moroccan traveller, ibn Battuta, enthused about it, declaring it 'the pleasantest and most beautiful town in Yemen. Its inhabitants are charming in their manners, upright and handsome, and the women are

The view of Mocha from the British Factory where George Annesley stayed. 'The best houses are all facing the sea, and chiefly to the north of the sea gate ... The town of Mocha is surrounded by a wall, which towards the sea is not above 16 feet high, though on the land side it may in some places be 30 feet. Two forts are erected for the protection of the harbour.' *AnnesleyII.17*

Above: 'Mocha, with its white chunamed, flat-terraced houses, and minarets interspersed with occasional date-trees, has rather a pretty appearance, particularly from the sea.' Drawn by Mrs Elwood's husband, Lt Colonel Elwood.   *Elwood 347*

Below: A mosque dominates the circular Tihamah houses at Musa. Men are praying on the rooftop of the stone house, while a man on a charpoy smokes his water-pipe. *AnnesleyII.362*

exceedingly beautiful.' He described the season of the colouring and ripening of the dates. 'Not a soul remains in the town, whether of the townsfolk or of the visitors. The musicians go out [to entertain them], and the shopkeepers go out selling fruits and sweetmeats.' In the 1760s, the German member of the Danish expedition to Yemen, Carsten Niebuhr, found the walls ruined, and a small citadel the only remaining fortification.

In July 1836, while the East India Company's surveying brig *Palinurus* was at Mocha making a plan of the roadstead, Lt. Charles J. Cruttenden, accompanied by the surgeon of the *Palinurus*, Dr. Jessop Hulton, took the opportunity to travel as far as Sana'a. The party also consisted of two servants who were their interpreters, and four muleteers. Their journey took them through Zabid, which they found of 'moderate size, not quite so large as Mokha ... and had a peculiarly gloomy appearance, owing to the dark colour of the brick with which the houses are built, and the ruinous state of many of them ... The Arabs have a tradition that it has been three times washed away by floods, with the exception of the Mesjid al-Jami', or principal mosque, which certainly wears a venerable appearance.'

The Italian, Renzo Manzoni, in the 1870s depicted the bazaar in Zabid as the finest in Yemen, and well stocked with local produce. Cruttenden pointed out that the principal articles of trade in Zabid and Bayt al-Faqih 'are piece goods from India, consisting chiefly of coarse blue and white cloth, English shawls, which are in great request, spices from Java, and sugar from Mauritius, which are bartered for money, wax, gums and frankincense and a

A large round watchtower stands out on the route between Mocha and Musa, with a few circular thatched huts. *AnnesleyII.361*

Above: Panorama of Hodeidah on the Red Sea, lying on the north-east side of a large bay.
Manzoni 356

Below: Bayt al-Faqih, situated on a sandy plain, was an important centre of trade. The fortress commands an incline to the left. The town lies approximately four days' journey from the triangle of Luhayyah, Mocha and Sana'a and is only one day's journey from the coffee hills, and coffee dealers from the Middle East and India came to buy.
Niebuhr(2)Pl.LXI

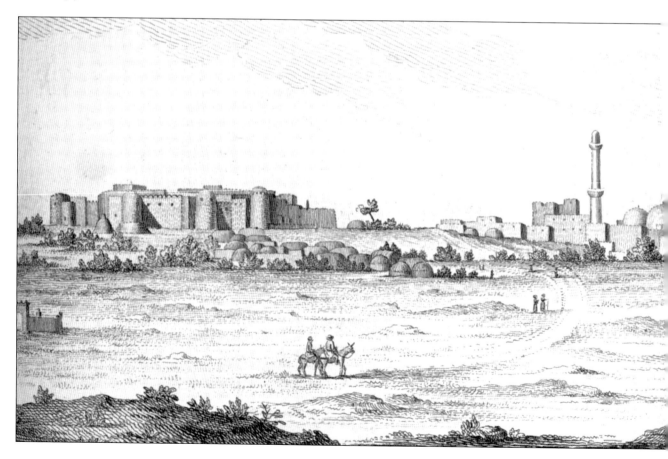

small quantity of coffee that the Bedawis bring down in preference to sending it to the Sana'a market.' Bayt al-Faqih, 'the emporium for all the coffee that comes from the interior,' Cruttenden and Hulton found was a large town of '8,000 persons with a citadel of some strength in the centre of it. The town itself was unwalled and consisted generally of a large kind of house, built partly of brick and partly of mud, and roofed with branches of the date-tree.' The French naval officer, de Grandpré, remarked that the principal support of the market of Bayt al-Faqih were three different caravans: 'The Persians flock to the market of Bethlefakih and form there the caravan of Bassora [Basra]. The coffee, which is distributed through Natolia [Anatolia], Turkey in Europe, and part of Russia, goes by way of Smyrna and joins the caravan of that name, while that which is intended for the coast of Barbary, and for Africa in general, joins the caravan of Cairo.'

The peoples of the Tihamah – a mixture of races – made their livelihoods from farming, fishing, date cultivation, pearl diving and salt production, indigo dyeing, pottery and brick making. The women wove baskets from palm fronds and embroidered. Niebuhr, travelling through Wadi Zabid, noted that 'the fields had a beautiful and rich appearance ... Much indigo is raised here; I counted more than six hundred large vessels in which the colouring matter is prepared for sale.'

Commerce was an important part of life. Trade routes ran north to south, one close to the sea, the other inland. The port of Luhayyah served the northern Tihamah. Tradition says Luhayyah was founded in the fifteenth century by a local saint around whose cell, and later tomb, the original settlement is said to have grown up. Niebuhr described the harbour as 'so indifferent', but added that: 'Notwithstanding this disadvantage, a considerable trade in coffee is carried on.' He remarked that 'several of the houses ... are built of stone; but the great part are huts ... The walls are of mud mixed with dung; and the roof is thatched with a sort of grass which is very common here.' James Bruce, the Scottish explorer, sailed south off the coast of the Red Sea on 18 July 1769, and he wrote 'at seven in the morning, we first discovered the mountains, under which lies the town of Loheia.' Provisions were plentiful

and reasonable, but the water was bad: 'it is found in the sand at the foot of the mountains, down the sides of which it has fallen in the time of rain, and is brought to the town in skins upon camels.' The bedouin sold fruit, milk and firewood. Bruce considered the government of the Imam 'much more gentle than any Moorish government in Arabia or Africa.' He also thought the people were 'of gentler manners'.

In the first century AD, Musa, which developed much later into the renowned coffee port of Mocha, was of great importance as a market town. The unknown author of *The Periplus* recorded that although there was no harbour, it did have a 'good roadstead and anchorage because of the sandy bottom.' The imports were 'purple cloths ... clothing in the Arabian style ... saffron, sweet rush, muslins, cloaks, blankets ... sashes of different colours, fragrant ointments.' Amongst the exports were 'selected myrrh, and the Gebanite-Minaean stacte, alabaster.'

Mocha was the chief port of South Tihamah. Its foundation in the fourteenth century is attributed to Ali ibn Umar al-Shadhili, a famous local hermit. In May 1609, the Englishman from Lyme Regis, John Jourdain, recounted: 'This cittie of Moucha standeth hard by the waters side in a plaine sandye field. It hath in it very faire buildings ...' and because the town was 'unreasonable hotte', he noticed that the people 'make howses of caves [sic] on the tops of their howses to take the aire.' In 1616 the Dutch Admiral, Pieter van den Broecke, was denied permission by the Ottoman Pasha to establish a factory in Mocha although he was given a coat of gold brocade. He noted that in the roadstead there were 'more than thirty Indian, Persian and Arab ships large and small.' At the close of the seventeenth century a commercial revolution was brought about which caused widespread ramifications in Yemen – the transit trade in spices was replaced by the local production of coffee. International commercial relations were greatly altered, and Yemen became the vital link. Yemeni coffee was purchased almost exclusively with gold and silver, and a great many ships were used to convey it from the Tihamah ports of Mocha, Hodeidah and other smaller ports to Jedda where it was taken by caravan and ship to Aleppo, the Maghreb, Egypt and beyond. Mocha was not only the principal port for the export of coffee, but was itself the general emporium of trade with Sana'a, Mecca, Cairo, Alexandra and India.

Left: **A soldier stands guard outside the Governor's house at Hodeidah.** *NicholsonPl.XIII*

Right: **A fort on the south side of Hodeidah flying the Turkish flag.** *NicholsonPl.XI*

Above: The port of Qunfidah on the Red Sea, northern Tihamah, in the 1830s. The gateway to the town, with coffee shops along the shore. James Bruce in the 1760s described Qunfidah as 'a small village, consisting of about 200 miserable houses, built with green wood, and covered with mats, made of the doom, or palm-tree; lying on a bay, or rather a shallow basin, in a desert waste or plain ... Nothing grows on shore excepting kelp, but it is exceedingly beautiful, and very luxuriant; farther in, there are gardens. Fish is in perfect plenty; butter and milk in great abundance.'   *NicholsonPl.XVII*

Below: View of Luhayyah in the 1760s from the sea: the buildings are made in stone and the huts with rounded roofs are made of grass.   *Niebuhr(2)I.Pl.XVI*

The British nobleman George Annesley, Viscount Valentia, stayed at the British Factory whilst in Mocha on his expedition to the Red Sea in the first decade of the nineteenth century, and found it 'tolerably handsome as all the buildings are whitewashed.' The outstanding engravings of the Tihamah, contained in his book, were struck by his secretary and draftsman, Henry Salt, and are represented in this volume. The Frenchman, Monsieur de la Grandpré, mentions the 'two European lodges or factories at Mocha, one for the French and one for the English; and each nation has the privilege of having its own flag over its appropriate habitation. That belonging to the French is a very poor building, of which the warehouses only are good, but the English one is handsome.' The French merchants, who had come to open trade in Yemen for the first time in the early 1700s (of whom Jean de la Roque wrote), appreciated the soldiers who patrolled the town and port to prevent 'disorders and thieveries – for in this country they are very zealous for the public quiet and good relations.' They estimated the population of Mocha to be 10,000 almost all 'Mohammedans, with some Armenians and a great many poor Jews in a separate quarter.'

Mrs. Anne Katherine Elwood, a British passenger on board ship to India in the 1820s together with her husband who made a sketch of Mocha, noticed: 'The women here [Mocha] were closely veiled, but they seemed to enjoy as much liberty as in any European town, and in the square upon which one of our windows looked [from the British Residency] we frequently saw them walking about, or conversing together in little knots. I believe they have the privilege of divorcing their husbands whenever they please, always retaining their marriage portion.' She added 'many of the houses are richly ornamented with highly finished cornices, fretwork, and other arabesque minarets, from whence the Muezzin calls the faithful to prayer, are extremely handsome.'

Early in the eighteenth century the Imam of Yemen allowed the Dutch, English, French and later the Americans to set up factories at Mocha, trading principally in coffee. A British Resident lived there more or less continuously from 1802 to 1830, and as early as 1828 the British established a coaling station to fuel the furnaces of steam ships on the India to Suez route. Aden, however, was far superior as a port, and as it developed in the nineteenth century the trade of Mocha died away. Cruttenden, Hulton and their party stayed in caravanserais on their journey and were supplied morning and evening with 'curdled milk and a coarse cake of Jowari [sorghum] bread, which weighs about a pound ...The whole cost of supper, breakfast, and a

night's lodging, did not exceed a third of a dollar, or ls. 6d. ... At this time grain had risen greatly in price, owing to the continued drought that had prevailed for nearly four years.' The party witnessed the horrific effects of famine: 'scenes of misery and wretchedness' on their passage across the Tihamah. 'In Mocha it was no uncommon thing to see dead bodies lying unheeded in the streets ... and this, added to the grinding tyranny and brutal oppression of the Egyptian troops, rendered the condition of these poor people almost insupportable.' In 1890, Walter Harris lamented that from a distance Mocha still 'has the appearance of being a flourishing town, but on nearer approach one can see that ... Mocha is today little more than a vast ruin.'

Hodeidah, north of Mocha, grew in importance and it became the chief Turkish base on Yemen's Red Sea coast, and port of entry. By the middle of the nineteenth century Yemen was going through a state of chronic economic depression – coffee was no longer its source of wealth because it had to compete with the lower-priced products of Ceylon, the West Indies, Java and later Brazil. Hodeidah attracted what little external commerce there was which had not been diverted to Aden – and Mocha lay silent.

Mrs. Elwood also wrote of her visit to Hodeidah and 'the exquisite beauty of the carved wood-work. The costume of the common women here [Hodeidah] appears to be composed of the blue cotton shift and veil and the superior orders seem to wear the Turkish drawers, vest, turban and veil.' She was fortunate to be invited into the houses and meet the women. In the evenings she would remain in her room in her husband's absence, but one evening she went on to the terrace to enjoy the fresh sea breeze. She was waved to and beckoned by several women to come and join them, as their husbands were 'all out of the way.' A young boy led her into a 'small interior court, at the door of which were a number of women's slippers, and inside were about a dozen females clothed in silk trousers, vests closely fitting the figure, and fastening in front, and turbans very tastefully put on.' She was received with 'the utmost cordiality and delight, the principal lady Zaccara making me sit down by her side – offering me coffee, which was brought on a silver tray in the usual beautiful little china cups.'

The women 'were amazingly struck with my costume, which they examined so minutely – what most amused them was the circumstance of my gown fastening behind. They asked me the names of every thing I had on, and when, to please them I took off my cap, and let down my long hair, Zaccara immediately took off her turban and showed me hers.'

Walter Harris took up 'his quarters' in Hodeidah 'which faced the sea on one side, and the only wide street in the town on the other.' He watched the 'scenes of character' from his second storey window and sauntered around the bazaars where he would sit talking to the Arab shopkeepers and sip coffee. 'All the nationalities of the world seemed to crowd there.' He enjoyed his hour or two in the afternoons with a bookseller from Zabid, who was good company, and pointed out 'the strange figures amongst the passers-by' – Jews, Indians of all kinds, Persians, Arabs, Egyptians, Bedouins, Abyssinians, Turks, Greeks, Negroes, and a few Europeans, 'would jostle each other in the narrow ways.' In the cafés Harris saw too 'the merchants, gorgeous in silk raiment and turbans talking business over coffee and tobacco.' He said that 'the greatest disadvantage ... after its feverish climate, is the exceedingly poor water-supply ... It is carried in skins and barrels on the backs of camels and donkeys ... But few Europeans live in Hodeidah, with exception of the Greeks. The wife of the British Vice-Consul was the one English lady in the place.'

Previous page: **The mosque at Luhayyah on the Red Sea with a *mu'ezzin* calling the faithful to prayer from its minaret. A woman carries a water pot on her head in the entrance to the huts, which are made from grass and wood. Outside, men sit on charpoys smoking water-pipes. A caravan arrives on the right. Illustration drawn on stone by W. Giles from a sketch by Captain C. Head.** *Head 6*

7

THE ISLANDS

Socotra: Hadibu with the Haggeher mountains behind (detail).
Head 6

Yemen's Red Sea islands are scattered for nearly 300 miles between Midi in the north and Bab al-Mandab Strait in the south. From the deep central trough rises the island of Jebel Zuqar, the largest of the volcanic group which includes the Hanish islands. Many of the uninhabited islands and islets are visited by fishermen, who also search for oysters and turtles. Some fishermen come from as far away as Mukalla. These islands served as safe anchorages for vessels plying the difficult waters, particularly before lights and beacons were erected in the Red Sea in the 1800s. Many are frequented by migratory birds on their arduous journeys to and from Africa. Almost every known form of coral reef is represented in the Red Sea.

Since the early centuries bc, Yemen and Ethiopia had close commercial relations, trading through Ethiopia's ancient port of Adulis in the Bay of Zulla and through other ports on the African and Arabian coasts. The Red Sea was criss-crossed by merchants – some of whom settled, along with other travellers, on either side and on its islands. In the sixth century, when the Persians gained command of the Red Sea and Aden, with its neighbouring ports, they also took possession of the Red Sea islands.

Opposite: **Fort on Kamaran Island.**   *NicholsonPl.XV*

Below: **A tall ship passes through the Bab al-Mandab Strait (Gate of Tears), between the Red Sea and the Gulf of Aden.**   *Irwin 11*

Kamaran

Off the Salif peninsula, which is well-known for its salt deposits, lies the island of Kamaran. Its north-east coast is fringed with mangroves, while coral reefs border its south coasts. A considerable expanse of deep water between Kamaran and the mainland forms a large natural harbour which is sheltered by the island.

From 1513 to 1517 the Portuguese attempted to occupy strategic places in order to take control of trade in the Red Sea. During their expeditions they put in at Kamaran with disastrous results: they were struck down by disease, heat and bad food. Meanwhile the Mamluks in Egypt wished to thwart the aspirations of the Portuguese by conquering Yemen and in 1515 their troops under Salman al-Rumi and Husayn Turki arrived at Kamaran. A Hadhrami chronicler wrote in 1515-16 that the Mamluks had 'come to fight the Frank' and they asked Amir bin Abd al-Wahhab, the last Taharid Sultan of Yemen if he would assist them 'in the way of victuals and money', but

Sultan Amir refused. The Mamluks threatened to attack him and were supported by the Zaydis on the mainland who promised supplies and horses. Eventually the Mamluks beheaded the Sultan near Jebel Nuqum in the vicinity of Sana'a. The well-known twentieth-century scholar, Robert Serjeant, who translated numerous Hadhrami manuscripts into English, commented that: 'It is stated by all Yemeni historians that the Taharid monarch Amir b. Abd al-Wahhab, was defeated by the fire-arms of the Mamluk forces which, till then, had been unknown in southern Arabia.' The Hadhrami chronicler added: 'The Egyptians built a fort and a mosque in Kamaran and they prayed the *Id al-Adha*, the 'Feast of the Sacrifices.'

During the pearling season, usually February to September, divers go out in canoes and dhows to the pearling banks. There they stay as long as food and water last. In the morning the men fish for oysters, and during the heat of the afternoon, shaded by the sails of their boats, they relax by playing musical instruments and singing. The oysters are taken to Kamaran where each shell is opened in the hope of finding a pearl. The pearls are then sorted and weighed by the merchants and exported. Another way of making a living was the netting of brilliantly-feathered singing birds, which landed on the island and which were sold or exchanged for fish.

In order to halt the progress of cholera, the International Sanitary Conference at Constantinople decided in 1866 that stricter quarantine measures must be imposed in the Red Sea concerning the pilgrimage to Mecca. Kamaran was occupied by the Turks from 1882 to 1915 as part of their province, and it was not until 1882, when there was a serious epidemic in the Hejaz, that pilgrims returning to Yemen were detained in a hastily-improvised quarantine station at Kamaran. That year there were 9,067 pilgrims. Pilgrim ships travelling to the Hejaz from places to the east of the Bab al-Mandab Strait had to stop at Kamaran and be dealt with according to the tenets of successive International Sanitary Conventions. The Constantinople Board of Health administered the station on behalf of the Ottoman Government during its occupation of the island. In 1884 the British Government appointed a member of the Indian Medical Service to be Vice-Consul at Hodeidah, a post which involved supervision of the Quarantine Station. A few years later a water condenser was installed near the village of Kamaran. Tombstones, with carved turbans under Ottoman influence, stand as memorials to the Turks who died during the Turkish occupations.

Perim

At the southern end of the Red Sea in the Bab al-Mandab Strait, called the 'Gate of Tears' because of its treacherous winds and currents, is the island of Perim. It is known as Mayun by the Arabs and as Diodorus in *The Periplus of the Erythraean Sea.*

'The great [Portuguese Commander] Afonso Dalboquerque set sail out of the harbour of Camarao [Kamaran] for India and without touching land anywhere, steered his course direct to the gates of the straits [Bab al-Mandab, south of the Red Sea].' He wanted to find out what islands there were and the harbours in them. 'One day, therefore, before sunrise he got into his boat all together in a party', with the pilot and others, and made his way into Perim harbour which looks towards the land of Prester John, Ethiopia. '...

the mouth of the harbour being so situated that when it has been entered the land appears to close in around it in such a manner that the open sea can no longer be seen.' Albuquerque and his party disembarked and explored much of the island. They found it 'covered with loose stones, large and small, with not a single tree, nor a green blade of grass in it.' A very ancient cistern and a pond were both 'choked up' but without water. Albuquerque ordered that a cross 'should be set, large and very tall, formed out of a mast and he inscribed upon it the name Ilha da Vera Cruz (Island of the True Cross) in remembrance of the cross he had seen in the sky', above the land of Prester John.

Over two hundred years later the invasion of Egypt by Napoleon in 1798 was seen by the British Government and the East India Company as a potential threat to their interests. One of their first defensive measures was to occupy the island of Perim on 3 May 1799 – an occupation that lasted only a few months. Lt Col. Murray, Commanding Perim, informed the Hon. J. Duncan Esquire Governor of Bombay in a letter dated 8 June 1799 that 'every exertion has been made to procure water on the island, but hitherto without a shadow of success – wherever we dig we find the soil perfectly salt and at a small depth a coral Rock'. Water had therefore to be brought from the mainland. Lt Col. Murray, convinced of the disadvantages of Perim, was directed by the Governor of Bombay to evacuate the island.

Nearly sixty years later, the British re-occupied the island. On 27 August 1856 the Political Resident Aden wrote a report to the Secretary to the Government in Bombay stating that Perim's position was important. The harbour is 'capacious and safe, and a light on the island would greatly facilitate the navigation of the Straits.' He continued: 'Perim in our hands would extinguish the extensive Slave traffic now carried on between Zailah, Tajourra, the Zanzibar Coast and the Ports of Yemen; a small inexpensive Naval Establishment at that point would suffice to watch the Straits and search every Vessel passing either way.' To emphasise the urgency of lighting the Red Sea, he added: '... steamers of the Peninsular and Oriental Company make two or three voyages up and down monthly; the Australian line will shortly commence operations and the Mauritius Company promises to extend to Suez; it will be no small boon to have the Straits well lighted so that vessels may pass at all hours of the night.'

An American ship brought news to the Aden authorities in December 1856 that a French brig was on its way from Zanzibar with orders to occupy Perim. The British responded speedily by hoisting the Union Jack over the island in January 1857, and installed a garrison.

In 1861 a lighthouse, burning coconut oil, was erected on Perim's northern bluff to the west of the island. The port of Aden lost much of its coaling business when the Perim Coal Company was given concessionary rights to set up a coaling station on the island in 1883 – a cut-throat competition between Aden and Perim lasted for many years. The most important factor in Perim's success was its deep, well-sheltered harbour which provided easy access to ships. Shipping increased with the opening of the Suez Canal in 1869. After a period of sheer desperation over the question of which department should pay for the much-needed dredging of Aden's harbour, operations finally began in 1891 and continued. It was then that the Perim Coal Company faced financial difficulties and the Company withdrew from the island in November 1936 when Perim port was closed to shipping.

The pearl fisheries of the Red Sea, particularly those around Perim, were exporting their produce through the port of Aden, and this formed a large part of Aden's export trade.

Hadibu with the magnificent Haggeher mountains behind.   *Head 2*

Socotra

Yemen's important and unique island of Socotra lies in a small archipelago where the Gulf of Aden enters the Indian Ocean and the Arabian Sea. Socotra is the most easterly and the largest of this group of islands. Its other members are The Brothers, frequently called The Sisters by early navigators (Samhah and Darsa), and Abd al-Kuri, the westernmost island. The history of the island goes back into mythology. It has long been linked with Pa'nch, the home of the King of the Incense Land and the legendary tale of the phoenix lying down to die in a nest scented by cinnamon and frankincense sprigs. It is considered that the name Socotra came originally from a Socotri word although it has also been suggested that it is derived from the Sanskrit, *Dvipa Sukhadhara*, or 'Isle of the Abode of Bliss', which was used by the Indians. A substantial trade existed between India and South Arabia, including Socotra, and lasted for thousands of years.

Another suggestion is the connection with Castor and Pollux, the *Dioscuri*, twin sons of Jupiter and Leda, from which the Roman name *Dioscoridis Insula* is said to have derived.

Dragon's Blood trees at Yehazahaz. 'The glory of Mount Haghier is undoubtedly its Dragon's Blood tree *(dracaena cinnabari)* found scattered at an elevation of about 1,000 feet and upwards over the great part of Sokotra. Certainly it is the quaintest tree imaginable, from 20 feet to 30 feet high.' *Bent(1)387*

Dracaena cinnabari, the Dragon's Blood tree, is still called by the Arabs *dam al-akhwein* – 'the blood of the two brothers'. Its resin is used by women to paint their faces, also as a medicine and to decorate the traditional Socotri pottery. It was sought-after in the rest of the world as a lacquer for furniture and certain musical instruments.

The unknown author of the *Periplus* called the island 'well out at sea' Dioscorida. 'The inhabitants are few … They are foreigners, a mixture of Arabs and Indians and Greeks, who have emigrated to carry on trade there.' Turtle shells of high quality and aloes were important articles of commerce in addition to frankincense and Dragon's Blood resin. Greeks and Indians settled on the island, adopting the language and customs. In the sixth century AD, the Graeco-Egyptian, Cosmas Indicopleustes, visited Socotra and thought the Greek-speaking people had been placed in 'Dioscorides' by the Ptolemies. Marco Polo in the thirteenth century remarked upon the harpooning of whales around its coasts for sperm-oil and ambergris and Duarte Barbosa, the Portuguese merchant adventurer, in the early sixteenth century noted the 'amber of good quality' to be found on Abd al-Kuri.

The islanders were Christians for centuries. Theodore Bent believed they were converted during the Ethiopian occupation, Marco Polo that they were Nestorians subject to their patriarch in Asia, and St Francis Xavier, visiting in 1541, recorded the

'The old capital Zoko [Suk] is a delicious spot, and the ruins are buried in groves of palm-trees by the side of a large and deep lagoon of fresh water … only separate from the sea by a narrow belt of sand and shingle … The view at Suk over the wide lagoon fringed with palm groves, on to the jagged heights of Mount Haghier rising immediately behind is, I think to be placed amongst the most enchanting I have ever seen.'   *Bent(1)394*

great veneration of the people for Saint Thomas. Padre Vincenzo, a Carmelite, visited the island in the seventeeth century and found the last traces of Christianity. 'The people still retained a perfect jumble of rites and ceremonies ... They had churches called moquamé, dark and dirty, and they daily anointed with butter an altar ... Each family have a cave where they deposited their dead.' Mr. and Mrs. Bent, at the end of the nineteenth century, discovered at the east of the island a curious form of ancient sepulchre. 'Caves in the limestone rocks have been filled with human bones from which the flesh had previously decayed ... Amongst the bones we found carved wooden objects which looked as if they had originally served as crosses to mark the tombs.'

The celebrated fifteenth century Arab navigator, Ahmed ibn Majid, stated that Socotra was in Mahri hands in 1488-9, and 'the Mashayikh of Mahra built a fort there and governed over some of its inhabitants, imposing unpaid labour on them, taking from each man a mound of ghee, and from each woman a rug of the weave of the country.' He also mentions that 'ruling over them is a woman, and as for marriage among them, it is in accordance to the advice of that woman, but in our time her power has ended and become weak.'

The Mahri appear to have been interested in the island because of their fear of the Kathiri Sultans of Hadhramaut, in particular the formidable Sultan Badr Bu Tuweirak, whose conquests are renowned in Hadhrami history. The Mahri, like the Shihri, have always been adventurous and enterprising sailors. The Portuguese rebuilt the Mahri fort in 1507 when Albuquerque captured Socotra with the intention of using the island as a depôt. They thought they could command the entrance to the Gulf of Aden and the Red Sea from Socotra before they discovered that it was Aden which was that entrance.

On 9 January 1834, after instructions from the British Government to interrupt his survey of the south coast of Arabia, Captain Stafford Bettewsorth Haines wrote to Lt. James Wellsted stating that it was 'the wish of Government to obtain all possible information regarding the Island,' with a view to using it as a base and coaling station that could be purchased from the Sultan of Qishn and Socotra, who lived in Qishn in Mahra, east of Hadhramaut, as well as on Socotra. While Haines concentrated on the bays and anchorages, Wellsted and Lt. Cruttenden studied the country and people. The Government did not heed the advice given by the Medical Officer who stated that the conditions on the island would be detrimental to the health of the British force, and so the expedition proved to be disastrous: an advance party of the Royal Indian Marine, on landing, were drowned in the surf, and the men stationed on the island were 'in a sickly state' from fever which took a heavy toll. The survivors were evacuated. Haines then proposed that Aden be considered once again as a coaling station. In 1876 the Sultan of Qishn and Socotra agreed not to alienate any part of his possessions except to the British and in 1886 Sultan Ali bin Abdullah bin Salem bin Saad bin Afrar accepted a Protectorate Treaty.

'Sultan Salem of Sokotra, nephew of old Sultan Ali of Kishin, the monarch of the Mahri tribe,' whom the Bents had met on the mainland, governed the island as his uncle's deputy. 'He was a man of fifty, with a handsome but sinister face; he was girt as to his head with a many-coloured kefieh, and as to his waist a girdle supporting a finely inlaid Maskat dagger and a sword. His body was enveloped in a clean white robe, and his feet were bare.' The Bents listed words from the unwritten languages of Socotri and Mahri, and remarked: 'In subtlety of sound Sokotri is painfully rich, and we had the greatest difficulty in transcribing the words. They corkscrew their tongues, they gurgle in their throats, and bring sound from most alarming depths.' Mabel Bent guessed there were nearly '12 to

The plain of Eriosh 'is covered with purely Ethiopic graffiti, almost exactly similar to those we saw on the steps of the church and on the hillsides around Aksum in Abyssinia.'
Bent(1)354

13,000 souls' on the island in 1897. Near Saihon, to the east, the Bents found the inhabitants friendly and were invited into their houses. They watched the women grinding limestone to make the traditional Socotri pottery.

No scientific investigators visited Socotra until 1879-80, when its exploration was entrusted to a distinguished naturalist, Isaac Bayley Balfour of Edinburgh. He and his team devoted two months to hard research and gathered large collections of exceptional interest and importance. In 1881 two German scientists, Dr. George Schweinfurth and Dr. Riebeck, with two colleagues, contributed further vital knowledge as a result of their exploration and discoveries during some six weeks on the island. Whenever they met the people 'either in their own caves or houses, we found them friendly, and neither women nor children, took flight at our approach.' Schweinfurth felt that his botanical researches afforded him 'ample opportunity for general observation of the Socotran animals. The number of birds, saurians, snakes and conchylates, gave full evidence of the peculiar nature of the Socotran fauna.' He thought that the 'greater portion possessed more of the characteristics of the South Arabian than of the African continent.'

In the winter of 1898-9 a conjoint expedition was undertaken by W. R. Ogilvie-Grant of the British Museum and Dr. Henry O. Forbes of the Liverpool Museums which resulted in *The Natural History of Sokotra and Abd el-Kuri*, edited by Dr. Forbes being the report of the expedition, together with information from other available sources. Several of its illustrations appear in this volume. In the chapter, 'Narrative of the Journey', Henry Forbes wrote: 'On landing [on Abd al-Kuri] we found them a rather timid, poor and ill-nourished company. They spoke both Arabic and Sokotri ... they had no objections to offer to our going anywhere on the island we pleased ... The dwellings were extremely poor. All were more or less circular in shape ... composed of unhewn blocks of coral and rough conglomerate stone piled one upon the other.' The flat roof was composed of brushwood under a layer of clay, mats or skins. The dress of the men was an 'ordinary turban round the head from the forehead to the nape of the neck; a loose cotton jacket buttoned down the front, and cotton cloth, girt about the loins, hanging down to the ankles from a supporting belt; over the shoulder they carried an extra cotton cloth, whose fashionable pattern was red and white check. Of the women we got only a glimpse, but their principal garment was the long thobe, worn slightly open at the throat, reaching down to the ankles. Some of the men wore sandals, but the majority went about barefooted.' Forbes estimated the number of people on the island to be 40 to 60. He regretted that his short visit did not enable him to treat the poor people who complained 'that they suffered greatly from fever, induration of the liver and especially their children, from dysentery ... I administered quinine and ipecacuanha to several of those who were suffering the most, but some of the children were hopelessly ill.'

December 7, 1898, Socotra: 'We steamed slowly along the northern coast of the island with a brilliant moon overhead. In passing through Tamarida Bay we had a splendid view, against the clear sky of the opening day, of the towering pyramids and needles of the Haghier range, which here enclose a wide deep amphitheatre in which lie embowered among palms the white houses of Hadibu [formerly Tamara/Tamarida].' Captain MacArthur, commander of the *Elphinstone*, together with Henry Forbes and an interpreter, were conducted to visit the Sultan of Qishn and Socotra. At first the Sultan was suspicious but when he read the letters of introduction and heard that it was to be a scientific mission only and not a retributory visit, 'Sultan Salem ... mellowed considerably ... He accorded us permission to visit any part of the island we desired.'

Observations and collections were undertaken in these islands and illustrations made which greatly widened the knowledge of their natural history, anthropology, ethnology and history. In modern times, scholars are recording and studying the Socotri language which is traditionally unwritten.

Kuria Muria

Hundreds of miles to the east of Aden, and some 20 miles from the coast of Oman lying in the Kuria Muria Bay, are the five islands of Kuria Muria (often given varying names and spellings): Hasikiyya, the most westerly; Suda, which was once inhabited and is the second largest; Hallaniyya, the largest of the group which is inhabited; Jabaliyya, which has a few tombs on it; and Charzut, which appears in old Portuguese writings as 'Rodondo'. The conical peaks of the islands are in fact the tops of a mountain range now submerged. The author of the *Periplus* called the islands 'Zenobian' and said that there were seven. Professor Serjeant says: 'The name is considered to be the Hellenized form of the Arabic "Beni Zenab" or "Genab", a tribe who owned the neighbouring coast.' The islands were also known as Khuryan Muryan.

The famous twelfth century Arab geographer, al-Idrisi, recorded that the islanders who were then under the rule of Shihr lived poorly in winter, but during the sailing season made a moderate livelihood by voyaging to Oman and Yemen where they traded in turtle shell and very fine amber.

In a despatch dated 29 June 1836, Charles Malcolm, Superintendent Indian Navy, during his survey of the islands for a possible coaling station conveyed that the Kuria Muria 'have no resources within themselves, the few people who inhabit Haleena in all 23 souls. The Islands, nominally part of the Imam of Muscat's territory, were 'utterly destitute.' He added that the Imam 'seldom gives them a thought.'

Eight years later they were visited by a British naval officer, Captain Stephen G. Fremantle, who described the conditions of ten of the inhabitants on one side of Hallaniyya: four men, three women, and three children. 'They have no huts, scarcely any clothes. And subsist entirely upon fish. They dwell in the clefts of the rocks with no furniture whatever except a mat or two. They have no boats. They cannot read or write. They have no idea of time, dates or even their own ages. They merely keep account of the moon's age and revolution for religious purposes as they are staunch Mohammedans. They speak and understand Arabic and have also a language of their own, not intelligible to my interpreter. They smoke tobacco and are capital swimmers. They were all born on the island, and, although the men sometimes go to Muscat or Zanzibar or even Bombay, their tenacity of home is invincible. One man in reply to a question from me said: "It is our home, and as long as there is a fish to be caught on the island, we prefer it to all the comforts and luxuries of any other spot in the world."'

In 1853, a master of a merchant ship from Liverpool, Captain Ord, touched at the Kuria Muria islands. He noticed vast quantities of guano, a valuable fertilizer, spread over one or two of the islands. Ord instructed his solicitor to write to the Foreign Office suggesting that Britain should occupy these islands and remove all the guano. The Foreign Office, wishing to acquire it for crop cultivation, took steps to find out whether the Imam of Muscat would cede the islands to Britain. 'The matter of the existence of the guano should be sedulously kept entirely out of sight', saying only that Britain needed the islands as a coaling station between Bombay and Aden. The British consul to Zanzibar, wrote that the islands 'are considered by His Highness the Imam as a dependency of Oman ... were frequently claimed by various tribes on the Hadhramaut coast ... were well known to the Bourbon [La Réunion] and Mauritius people' and ships called there to take the guano; also Arabs from the Red Sea 'take many cargoes of it to Makalla and other ports.' They used it especially for cultivating tobacco. The British drafted a short Deed of Cession and on 14 July 1854 it was signed and sealed by Sultan Said bin Sultan of Oman with Fremantle as witness. In 1855 Captain Ord received a licence to remove the guano.

Captain Haines, the first British Political Agent in Aden, remarked that Hallaniyya 'is sometimes visited by a boat belonging to the Kulfan family of the Mahrah tribe, who claim the Kooria Mooria group as their hereditary property and the name by which they are known amongst the Islands of the family of Khulfan.' Sheikh Said bin Umar bin Ghalfan, the head of the tribe, retired temporarily to Hallaniyya, and on returning to the mainland kept possession of the islands. When in November 1883 Colonel Miles and Captain Long visited Hallaniyya they found less than 40 inhabitants, two women of the Beni Ghalfan were considered 'queens'. Nothing very much had improved for these poor people, who were 'subsisting on fish, shellfish and goat's milk, occasionally exchanging their dried fish for dates and rice with passing dhows ...The headman is Hamed bin Mubraek the only person who can speak Arabic, the rest speaking Mahra ... Between 200 to 300 goats were on the island, some being quite wild, while some were attended by women and children. They were gratified by being given a little sugar, rice, tobacco and cotton cloth.'

The islands were part of the British Colony of Aden. Being so remote from the Colony, they were put under the charge of the British Resident Persian Gulf, who did very little to help them. They are now, once again, part of the Sultanate of Oman and are today known as Juzur al-Hallaniyat.

8

FAUNA & FLORA

Note: The names in this section are given as in the works of the foreign travellers concerned, and no attempt has been made to include more recent scientific names.

Phalacrorax nigrularis 'In Gubbat Shoah, below Ras Beduwa, we saw a number of Cormorants swimming in the bay, some being entirely black and different from any we had seen … these Cormorants, both adult birds in full breeding plumage, belonged to a new species.' *ForbesPl.VI*

Mammals

Felix nimr, (leopards) in 'Arabia Felix'. Sadly many of these beautiful creatures were killed for their skins, which attracted high prices. It is uncertain if any now exist in Yemen. *Hemprich & EhrenbergPl.XVII*

146

Several of the travellers remarked that they had seen 'hundreds' or 'thousands' of baboons and heard the chattering and barking of males, females and young.
Hemprich & EhrenbergPl.XI

The ibex is the best known of South Arabia's wild animals and has never lost its legendary power to influence human life. Its horns were placed on new buildings as a protection against the Evil Eye, as one can see in many towns in Hadhramaut and other governorates. Until recent times a successful ibex hunt was cause for celebration. The returning hunters held aloft the horns of the ibex, some decorated with bells, and danced through the streets, shouting, clapping, rushing backwards and forwards or turning in circles. One man would play the part of the unfortunate ibex, while others would play the hunters. They would be followed by a crowd waving sticks or guns. The ibex is now a protected species and it is forbidden to hunt them.   *Hemprich & EhrenbergPl.XVIII*

Above: **The bat.** *Rüppell 18*

Below: 'The Jerboa is a small harmless animal of the desert, nearly the size of a common rat ... It lives in the smoothest plains or places of the desert, especially where the soil is fixed gravel, for in that chiefly it burrows, dividing its hole below into many mansions. It seems to be apprehensive of the falling in of the ground; it therefore generally digs its hole under the root of some spurge, thyme, or absinthium, upon whose root it seems to depend for its roof not falling in ... It seems to delight most in those places that are haunted by the cerastes, or horned viper. Nature has certainly imposed this dangerous neighbourhood upon the one for the good and advantage of the other.' *Bruce V.121*

Above: The wild asses of Socotra were described by Dr. Ogilvie-Grant as, 'remarkably sturdy, thick-set little animals, with beautiful clean legs and remarkably small hoofs.' Henry Forbes believed they were 'survivors of Nubian ancestors brought from the Red Sea coast by, probably, the ancient Egyptian incense collectors.'   *Forbes 18*

Below: The lynx has 'very much the appearance of the common cat. He is said to be exceedingly fierce, and to attack man if at any way pressed. At this time he mounts easily upon the highest trees; at other times he is content with hiding himself in bushes, but in the season of the fly he takes to holes and caverns in the ground.'   *Bruce V.146*

Above: The hyaena. 'There are few animals whose history has passed under the consideration of naturalists, that have given occasion to so much confusion and equivocation as the Hyaena has done. It began very early among the ancients, and the moderns have fully contributed their share ... His proper name is Dubbah, and this is the name he goes under among the best Arabian naturalists.'   *BruceV.107*

Below: Antelope: male, female and juvenile.   *Hemprich and EhrenbergPl.V*

Birds

Above: **Red Sea Herons. Adults and a juvenile, with eggs in front.**
Hemprich & EhrenbergPl.VI

Right: Pelicanus rufescens. **The Pelican.**
Rüppell Zoologie21

Top left: The Arabian bustard. 'Houbarra or houbaary is of the size of a capon, but with a longer body. It feeds upon shrubs and insects.' *Shaw 333*

Bottom left: 'Rhaad which denotes thunder ... from the noise it makes in springing from the ground.' *Shaw 333*

Above: Scops socotranus 'We spent a night in the Addah Valley to the east of the Hadibu plain, and it was there that we first heard the cry of this new species ... Each owl apparently had its own hunting ground and special trees on which it perched and uttered its cry ... The food appears to consist almost entirely of beetles.' *ForbesPl.V*

Left: Sheregig or Roller, 'a gorgeous blue' and seen 'wherever there are meadows, or long grass, interspersed with lofty or shady trees.' *BruceV.183*

Left: Passer Hemileucus. 'This sparrow was certainly one of the most interesting birds met with on Abd al-Kuri. It was never seen in the neighbourhood of the native village, but appeared to be confined to the bush-clad slopes of one of the highest points, where enormous limestone blocks which have fallen away from the summit lie scattered over the hillside. Here it makes its home ... they are very shy and not very numerous.' *ForbesPl.VII*

Right: Motacilla Forwoodi. 'Forwood's wagtail was only met with on the island of Abd el-Kuri, where it was common enough on the stony plain outside the native village.' *ForbesPl.VII*

Above: Caprimulgus jonesi. The only example of the Socotran nightjar was found in the Dimichiro Valley in the Garieh Plain, East Socotra. 'It was found squatting on the ground among the stones close to our rest-camp in the Valley ... We never came across the species on any other occasion.' *ForbesPl.IV*

Nests

Right: **Nest of** *cisticola incana.* 'This small Fan-tailed Warbler was common in almost all bush-clad parts of the island from nearly sea level to an elevation of at least 4,500 feet ... The beautiful dome-shaped structure, with an entrance at the side ... was built of fine grass, ornamented with patches of orange lichen, and placed in a thick bush about three feet from the ground ... When hopping about the bush these birds generally carry the tail in a semi-erect position. They are extraordinarily lively little creatures, constantly chattering and scolding, and chasing one another up and down the hillsides.'   *Forbes Fig.4*

Above: **Nest of** *Belenogaster Saussurei.* **A type of wasp,** 'not closely allied to any known species.' *Forbes 248*

Nest of *Fringillaria insularis.* 'The Bunting was common on all parts of the island of Socotra visited by us ... The females are much less frequently seen than the males ... The food consists chiefly of fine grass seeds and the seeds of various bushes ... The first nest [beneath a granite boulder] I saw was at Homhil [to the east of Socotra] ... It was situated close to the side of a goat track in thin Boxwood jungle interspersed with large Dragon's Blood trees, and consisted of a slight structure of twigs and grass stems, lined with finer grass, partially hidden by a small Boxwood bush at the root of which it was placed.'   *Forbes Fig.2*

Insects

Butterflies of Socotra.   1: *Charaxes balfouri* – female; 1a: the same, under surface; 2: *Tarucus socotranus* – female; 2a: the same, under surface; 2b: the same – male, upper surface; 3: *Tarucus quadratus* – female, upper surface; 3b: the same – male, upper surface; 4: *Belenois anomala* – female, upper surface; 5: *Rhopalocampta jucunda* – under surface; 5a: larva of same; 5b: front view of head of larva of same; 5c: pupa of same.   *ForbesPl.XIX*

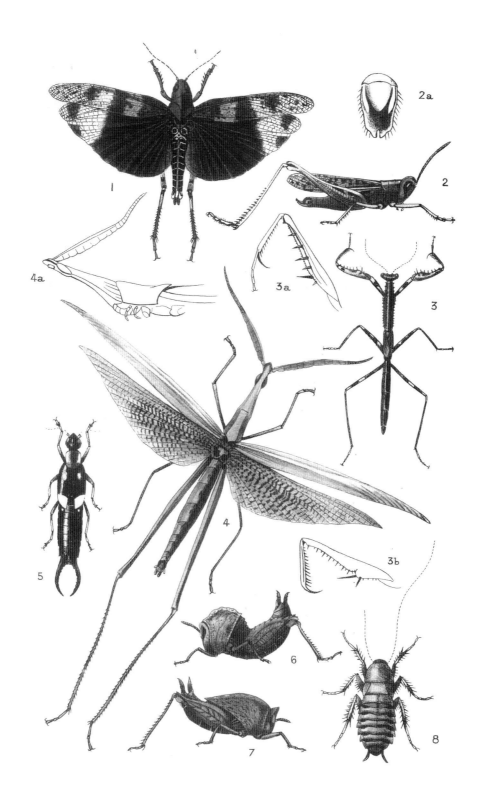

Earwigs, Grasshoppers and Crickets of Socotra.

1: *Dissosteira forbesii* – male; 2: *Cataloipus oberthuri* – female; 2a: the same – subgenital lamina – male; 3: *Teddia dopscpro*s – male; 3a: anterior foot, internal surface; 3b: anterior foot, external surface; 4 and 4a: *Truxalis ensis*; 5: Forficula smyrnesis – male; 6: *Plagiotypus granti* – female; 7: *Phaulotypus granti* – female; 8: *Loboptera peculiaris.*   *ForbesPl.XXV*

Reptiles

Above: Cerastes or Horned Viper. 'The Cerastes hides itself all day in holes in the sand, where it lives in contiguous and similar houses to those of the jerboa ... the reader will attend to the horn which is placed over the eye in the manner I have given the picture of it, it is fluted, and has four divisions. He will likewise observe the tooth as observed through a glass. He may suppose the black represents a painter's pallet, for the easier discerning the white tooth which could not otherwise appear distinctly upon white paper.' *Bruce V. 198*

Right: Phyllodactylus Riebeckii, **Large Gecko of Socotra, named after Dr. Riebeck, the German scientist.** *Forbes Pl. VIII*

Sea Creatures

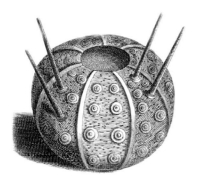

Above: Red Sea urchin.   *Shaw 324*

Right: Caretta, or sea-tortoise, also known as Hawk's bill tortoise.   *BruceV.215*

Below: Arnold von Harff's impression of a strange occurrence: 'On the voyage between Madach [Aden] and Schoyra [Socotra] we saw three times towards evening, in the sea, two mighty beasts fighting furiously ... one was a sea dragon ... and the other a whale.' *Groote 137*

Above: Red Sea shells. 'It is observed that pearls are always the most beautiful in those places of the sea where a quantity of fresh water falls. Thus in the Red Sea they were always most esteemed that were fished from Suakim southward ... on the Arabian coast, near the island Camaran, where there is abundance of fresh water.'   *Bruce 219*

Fish

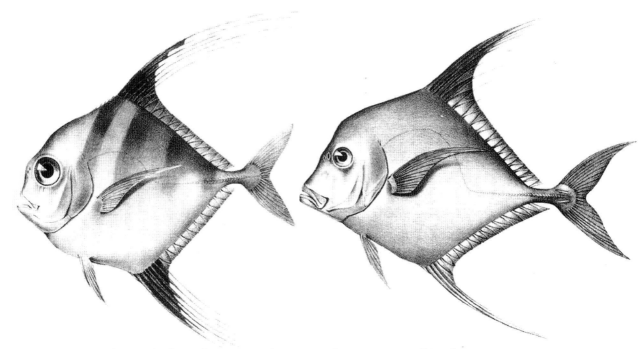

Above: **Blepharis fasciatus** *and* **Scyris indicus.**   *Rüppell Zoologie 33*

Above: **Holocentrus ruber, Holocentrus diadema, Holocentrus samora.**   *Rüppell Zoologie 22*

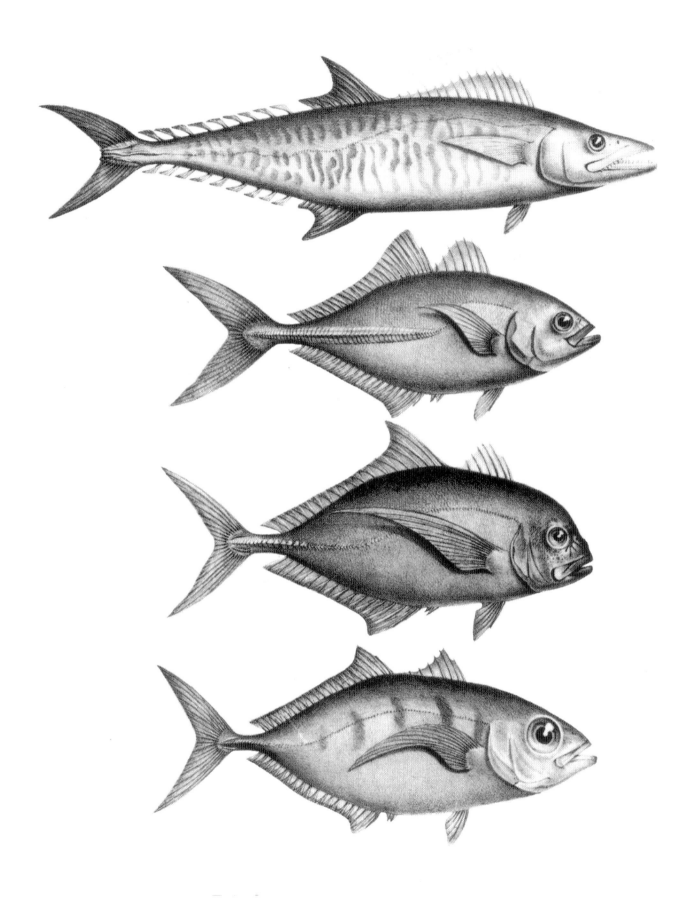

Caranx bajad, Caranx fedau, Caranx fulvoguttatus, and *Citula ciliaria.* *Rüppell Zoologie 25*

Flora

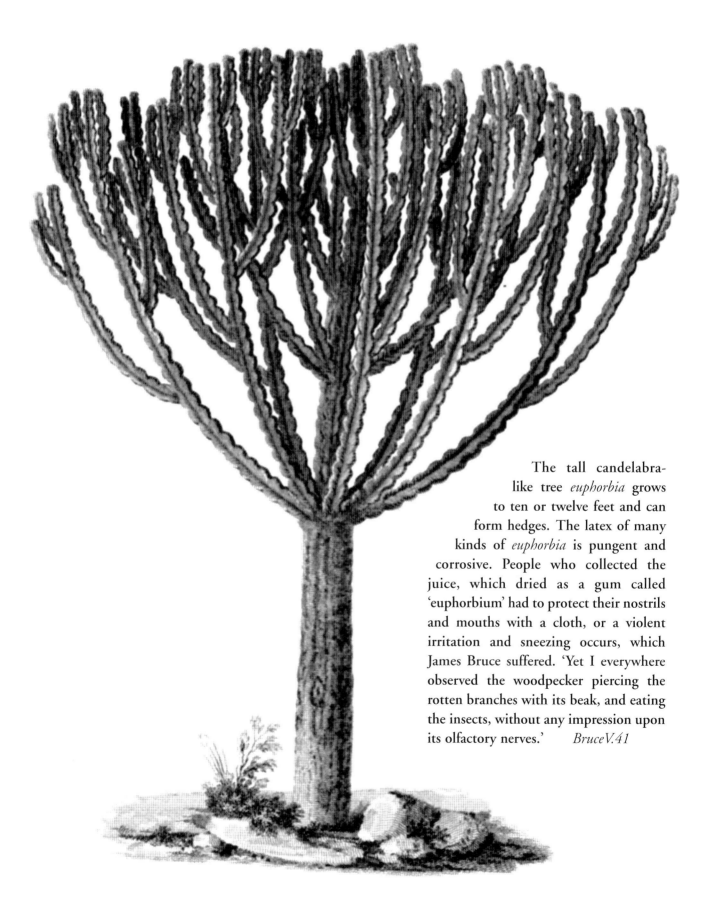

The tall candelabra-like tree *euphorbia* grows to ten or twelve feet and can form hedges. The latex of many kinds of *euphorbia* is pungent and corrosive. People who collected the juice, which dried as a gum called 'euphorbium' had to protect their nostrils and mouths with a cloth, or a violent irritation and sneezing occurs, which James Bruce suffered. 'Yet I everywhere observed the woodpecker piercing the rotten branches with its beak, and eating the insects, without any impression upon its olfactory nerves.' *Bruce V.41*

Left: The cucumber-shaped tree *Dendrosicyos* – 'a tree in many parts of the island of Socotra.' *Schweinfurth 617*

Below left: Adenium tree in bloom on Socotra – Schweinfurth admired 'the beauty of rose-red oleander blossoms.' *Schweinfurth 37*

Above: ***Dracaena cinnabari.*** A young Dragon's Blood tree, with flowering aloe on the left of it. *Schweinfurth 45*

164

Right: **Banana** – known as mauz **or** *muza* in Arabic. The whole plant is put to a variety of uses, from house building to cooking. It should 'not be pass'd over without Admiration'. *Ludolf Preface*

Left: Balsam tree, sometimes known in Hadhramaut as Hadhramaut myrrh. The tree, or shrub, grows widely in Yemen. Peter Forskal, the noted botanist on the Danish expedition in the early 1760s, found a specimen in full bloom in the mountains north-west of Ta'izz. Its resin is said to be oily and to taste like lemon and it is used as a chewing gum, but when burned as an incense it smells of India-rubber. *BruceV.16*

A branch of the frankincense tree – *Boswellia* species. The tree has a mass of branches with grey papery bark, and its tiny leaves give little shade. In late September, star-shaped flowers appear. Resin from the trunk of the tree was highly valued throughout the world in ancient times, and harvesting methods have scarcely changed since those times. *Carter*

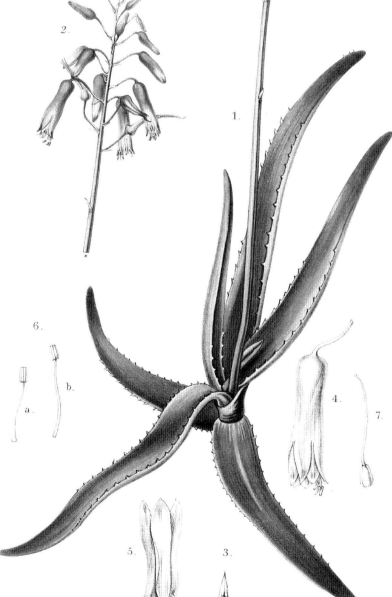

Left: Exacum forbesii – 'its sweet-scented flowers stand up nicely in small trusses above the foliage.'   *ForbesPl.XXVIA*

Right: Aloe forbesii. Aloe was formerly exported in large quantities from Socotra and is used in medicines and beauty products.   *ForbesPl.XXVIB*

A. Hyoscyamus datora. B. Parnassia polynectaria.   Forskal/NiebuhrPl.V

Left: Rack 'grows in abundance in Arabia Felix ... The Arabians, it is said, make boots of this tree. Its wood is so hardened by the sea, and also so bitter in taste, that no worm whatever will touch it. Of this tree the Arabians also make tooth-picks ... reputable to be favourable to the teeth, gums and breath.'   *Bruce V.44*

Right: Aspidopteris yemensis.   DeflersPl.I

Right: **The coffee shrub.**   *Roque 288*

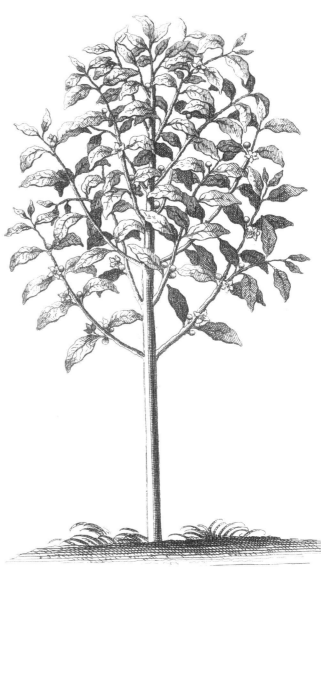

Above: **Glinus crystallinus.**   *Forskal/NiebuhrPl.XIV*

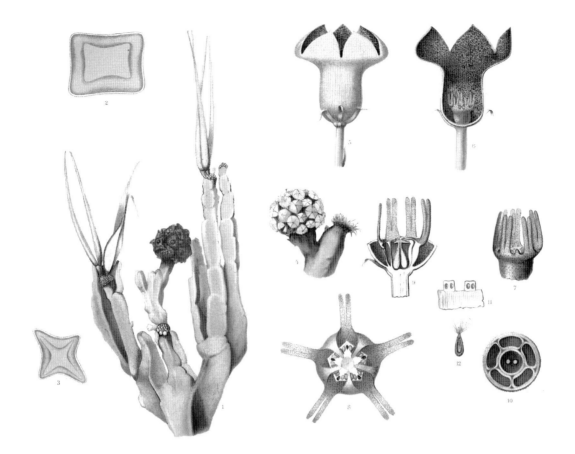

Above: **Boucerosia adensis deflers.**   *LoossPl.III*

Below: **Echnidnopsis quadrangular forskal.**   *LoossPl.II:*

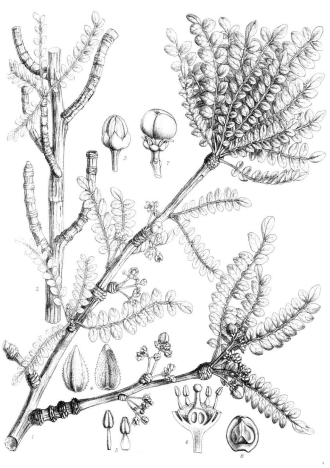

Left: Boswellia socotrana grows on the Haggeher mountains. It is a very distinct species, quite unlike any of the other species of the genus, both in foliage and flowers. Dr. Georg Schweinfurth remarked that the bark was used as tanners' bark. B*alfourPl.XI*

Right: Asplenium schweinfurthii.
BalfourPl.C

9

THE TRAVELLERS
& ARTISTS

James Bruce 1730-1794, Scottish traveller and artist.
ShawIN Frontispiece

Over the centuries Yemen became known to foreign merchant adventurers, invaders, traders, explorers and travellers, and the images that they and artists, draftsmen, photographers, publishers and printers have left us illustrate the magnificent scenic beauty, unique architecture and historical importance of the country. Many of the early Arab travellers were Muslims who journeyed through Yemen when making the pilgrimage to the holy cities of Mecca and Medina. A Yemeni historian, Omarah, who lived in the twelfth century, wrote that to a 'Just Ruler', one Husayn ibn Salamah, 'must be reckoned the construction of great mosques and lofty minarets along the road from Hadhramaut to the city of Mecca … The distance extends over sixty days' journey … The first stations were at Shibam and Tarim.' One of the most famous pilgrims and travellers was the fourteenth century Moroccan Mohammed ibn Abdullah ibn Battuta. In his *Travels* he wrote not only about the religious ceremonies, but also his impressions of the people he met and of the places he visited.

An early European traveller who claimed he had visited Yemen, was the Rhinelander, Arnold von Harff. In 1496 he wrote of his experiences in Arabia and asserted that he had visited the island of Socotra. His book is said to have been widely circulated in manuscript, and was first printed by Dr. Eberhard von Groote in 1860. Von Groote, the first editor, based his text on three manuscripts which aroused considerable interest in Germany, and made woodcuts of von Harff's drawings, which are used in this publication. Von Harff's drawings are unfortunately deteriorating.

In 1510, the first account of Sana'a by a European was published in Rome. The author, Ludovico di Varthema, described himself as 'of very slender understanding' and not given to study, but resolved to 'see things personally and with my own eyes.' He spent several months in jail on his arrival in Yemen because the Arabs were suspicious of any foreigners, suspecting they might be spies acting for Portuguese traders. When released, di Varthema succeeded in travelling into the interior and reached far up into the mountains around Sana'a.

The Arabs controlled much of the Indian and Far Eastern trade before the arrival of the Portuguese, who started their incursions into the Indian Ocean in the early 1500s and rapidly expanded their power and influence. They were active off the south Arabian coast and in the Red Sea. Afonso d'Albuquerque, Governor of the Portuguese settlements and factories in western India, failed in his attempt to take Aden in 1513. Towards the end of the sixteenth century the arrival of the English, and hard on their heels, the Dutch, broke the Portuguese monopoly of trade in the Indian Ocean.

In April 1609, during the first Turkish occupation of Yemen, the first British ship anchored before the 'castell' of Aden. John Jourdain, of Lyme Regis in England, and a merchant for the East India Company, asked permission to open a factory in Yemen, whereupon the Pasha replied that it could not be permitted 'without the expresse order from the Great Turke, his master.' Some years later, in 1618, Captain Shilling arrived in Yemen in the *Anne Royal* with a firman from the Ottoman Sultan, permitting the English to establish a factory.

In the early 1700s the Frenchman, Jean de la Roque, in his *A Voyage to Arabia Felix*, published in 1716 gives the account of French merchants who visited Yemen. The merchants, having arrived in Mocha, were conducted to the Governor's Palace where they had an audience with the Governor. He 'was seated upon two carpets

The Rhinelander, Arnold von Harff. *Groote 1*

174

embroidered with gold, leaning upon cushions ' They had come for 'the first time to open Trade in the Kingdom of Yaman' and to make 'A Treaty between the Governor of Moka and the Captains of the French ships, the sixteenth January 1709.'

The 1760s witnessed the first large-scale scientific expedition to Arabia, which was approved and financed by King Frederik V of Denmark. The party consisted of: Carsten Niebuhr, a German mathematician and surveyor; William Baurenfeind, a German artist; Peter Forskal, a Swedish botanist; two Danes, Friederich Christian von Haven, a philologist and Oriental scholar, and Christian Carl Kramer, a surgeon zoologist; and a Swedish servant, Berggren. The results of their ill-fated expedition and admirable labours contributed enormously to the knowledge of Yemen at that time and the wealth of engravings that resulted from their work enrich this volume. Niebuhr, the sole survivor of the Danish expedition, fought hard to publicise his colleagues' achievements and discoveries. Eventually he had to finance the publication of Forskal's work, which included Baurenfeind's drawings, from his own pocket – the State refused to contribute any money.

Several botanists visited Yemen in the nineteenth century. Unfortunately, very little survives of the diaries and reports of Ulrich Jasper Seetzen 'styled *"conseiller d'ambassade"* in the Russian service, who for twenty years had trained himself in Germany to be an eastern explorer', as the author David George Hogarth wrote, 1904. He was a learned Arabist and botanist whom Hogarth called 'a profound observer of things and men.' Seetzen made the journey to Mecca disguised as a Muslim. He visited Sana'a in 1810 and felt, after all the cities he had visited, that it was the finest he had seen, with its gardens and massive houses. Seetzen was murdered somewhere near Ta'izz. The Frenchman, Paul Emile Botta, physician to Mohammed Ali Pasha, was commissioned by the Natural History Museum of Paris. He arrived at Hodeidah in 1836 and succeeded in establishing good relations with the semi-independent chief of the district between Hays and Ta'izz. With this protection he was able to carry out his researches on the great Jebel Sabir, which was his main achievement. It was unfortunate that Peter Forskal had not been given permission to do this in the previous century. Another Frenchman, A. Deflers, carried out his botanical survey at the end of the 1880s and in the 1890s. Theodore and Mabel Bent's party included a botanist from Kew Gardens in London, William Lunt.

Mention should be made of the European travellers en route to Africa, India and China who illustrated their journeys. By the end of the eighteenth century it was not uncommon for West Europeans to journey overland through Egypt and Syria. They became interested in the lands which bordered the Red Sea, and as the nineteenth century progressed some longed for further adventure and exploration. The opening of the Suez Canal in 1869 was seen as uniting East and West. A number of vessels of the big steamship companies began to carry passengers, and the numbers increased dramatically by the end of the nineteenth century. British officials seconded from India to serve in Aden brought with them their Anglo-Indian architecture, and introduced mulligatawny soup with rice for breakfast on Sundays. Their principal communication with 'home' was the Peninsula and Oriental Steam Navigation Line [P&O], whose ships arrived early on Sunday mornings. An official travelling to or from India, according to his status, was given a cabin on the 'Portside Out and Starboard Home', thus enjoying the cooler side of the ship, and giving a new word to the English language – POSH. Men and women passengers recorded their experiences and journeys in writing and pictures some of which were published in books and also appeared in such periodicals as *The Illustrated London News* and *The Graphic*. A British woman passenger named Anne Katherine Elwood travelled with her husband, Colonel Elwood, to India overland from England through Europe, Egypt and across the Red Sea during the years 1825-28. She wrote in letters and a journal to her sister who had asked for an account of the Elwoods' journey 'and probably mine was the

Far left, top: **William Baurenfeind, from South Germany, was an artist and engraver and a member of the Danish expedition of 1761-3. He died on board ship from Mocha to Bombay.**
Paul Hamilton, Seas of Sand 1971

Far left, bottom: **Peter Forskal 1732-1763, the Swedish botanist. He was a member of the Danish expedition to Yemen, 1761-63, and died at Yarim.** *Forskal Frontispiece*

Left: **The German mathematician and astronomer, Carsten Niebuhr (1733-1815), dressed in Arab costume given to him by the Imam of Sana'a. He was a member of the Danish expedition to Yemen in 1761-63. This expedition gathered the most important and remarkable information about the country and its people known at that time. Niebuhr's work contains the first comprehensive collection of engravings of Yemen.**
Niebuhr(2)I.Pl.LXXI

first Journal ever kept by an English woman in the Desert of Thebais and on the shores of the Red Sea.'

Many of the foreign travellers journeying to and from East Africa would disembark in Aden to arrange their onward voyage. Amongst them was the famous British orientalist Sir Richard Burton who came in 1854 *en route* to Harar in Ethiopia. In the previous century, James Bruce, the Scottish explorer and talented artist, embarked on his historic journey to 'discover' the source of the Blue Nile in 1769. He and Luigi Balugani, his Italian assistant, using a camera obscura, drew many sketches. Sadly most were lost on Bruce's return journey. The engravings concerning Yemen are to be seen in the preceding pages. In the first decade of the nineteenth century, the distinguished British draftsman and envoy, Henry Salt, whose attention to detail afforded an in-depth study of the architecture, places and people. His engravings have long been sought-after by collectors. Illustrations of Aden are reproduced in this volume by the German artist, Johann Bernatz, who spent time in Aden before accompanying Captain Sir William Cornwallis Harris, the leader of a British diplomatic mission, to Shawa in Ethiopia in the 1840s.

No less valuable are the images and writings of British officers who explored Yemen and carried out excellent and meticulous surveys of its interior and coast, and whose creative achievements appear in this work. Not only did they have notepads to hand but also their sketchbooks or other material to illustrate their findings. One Captain Charles

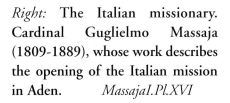

Right: **The Italian missionary. Cardinal Guglielmo Massaja (1809-1889), whose work describes the opening of the Italian mission in Aden.** *MassajaI.Pl.XVI*

Renzo Manzoni, the Italian traveller who visited Yemen three times during 1877-80, and whose work forms the basis of a large collection of engravings on Yemen.
Manzoni Frontispiece

Franklin Head, of the Queen's Royal Regiment, intended to show 'the advantage and practicability of steam navigation from England to India' in the 1800s published in his splendid pictorial work in which W. Walton and W. Giles drew on stone Head's sketches of Hadibu in Socotra, together with Mocha and the mosque in Luhayyah, both in the Tihamah.

The energetic Italian traveller, Renzo Manzoni, visited Yemen in three visits from 1877 to 1880, during the rule of the self-proclaimed Imam al-Hadi Sharaf al-Din. Manzoni's descriptive accounts of the Turkish occupation, and of the Yemeni people and their country, are accompanied by copious detailed engravings. He was the first traveller to publish any photographs of Sana'a. A few years later, a British correspondent of *The Times* in Morocco, Walter Harris, described his journey through Yemen. Like Manzoni, he wrote of the Turkish occupation, although by his time Imam al-Hadi Sharaf al-Din had died (in 1890) and the *ulema* of the Imam's circle agreed to acknowledge al-Mansur billah Mohammed bin Yahya Hamid al-Din as the new Imam. The evocative views throughout his work are based on his sketches, some of which also appeared in *The Illustrated London News*. When Harris reached Manakha, on the Sana'a to Hodeidah road, he reported to the Turkish Government office. When his letters to the Governor had been presented, he was taken to meet the Kaimakan. On leaving the office he was followed by a guard 'who, however, did not in the least interfere with my actions, and in whose presence I was venturesome enough to sketch, without calling forth any sterner reproof than that if they were caught allowing me to draw they might get into trouble, so that I had better creep behind a rock and make my sketches I wanted from a spot where I would not be seen.'

An important contributor to the study of Hadhramaut in the 1880s was the Dutchman, L.W.C. van den Berg, an Arabic scholar. In view of the increasing Arab influx in the Dutch East Indian possessions, the Governor-General of the Dutch East Indies asked van den Berg to interview, research and write on the lives of the Arabs living in the archipelago, whose

Henry Salt, 1780-1827, the British envoy, was a distinguished draftsman. *HallsII Frontispiece.*

origins, in the main, stemmed from Hadhramaut. Although he was not a foreign traveller to Yemen, it is appropriate to include him in this collection because his researches on Hadhramaut among immigrant Arabs in the Dutch East Indies are remarkable for their completeness and general accuracy.

Hadhramaut encountered its first English woman in 1893. Mabel Bent accompanied her husband James Theodore Bent into the interior and to the towns in Wadi Hadhramaut and to other parts of Yemen. It was suggested to Bent that a survey of Hadhramaut by an independent traveller would be useful to the British Government. Mr and Mrs. Bent also visited Socotra 'with the object of trying to unravel some of its ancient history so shrouded in mystery.' Sadly Theodore Bent died 'four days after our return from our last journey there [Southern Arabia].' Mabel Bent explained that it was left to her to put 'the whole thing into as consecutive a form as possible, only saying that the least part of the writing is mine.' Her husband's artistry is a charming and poignant complement to this couple's work. In the obituary of Mabel Bent in the *Geographical Journal* of 1929, the year of her death, it read that she 'was his constant companion on these expeditions, sharing in all the dangers and hardships involved, and collaborating with him in the publication of their results.'

A number of travellers, including scholars and archaeologists, were interested in the ancient inscriptions of Yemen. They hoped they would be able perhaps to throw more light on the inscriptions and ruins of which Niebuhr had written in the 1760s. Lt. Cruttenden and Dr. Charles Jessop Hulton found inscriptions 'in the neighbourhood of the most ancient part of Sana'a' during their visit to the city. They copied four, said to be the first from the north of Yemen, although they were believed to be from the important site of Marib. Dr. Hulton died soon after the party rejoined the *Palinurus* at Mocha. 'In closing this brief Memoir of our journey into Yemen', wrote Cruttenden, 'I can only regret that the task has not fallen into abler hands than mine. I am well aware that an account drawn up by a man of such general attainments, and especially in geology, as Dr. Hulton, would have been far more valuable and

Georg Schweinfurth, 1836-1925, the German scientist, was described as a man who 'took a high place for his scientific attainments and for the breadth of his interests in many different fields of knowledge.
Mitteilungen aus den Deutschen Schutzgebieten, Hans Meyer, Berlin 1925 .

satisfactory.' Between 1843 and 1890, three European travellers reached Marib. Joseph Thomas Arnaud, a French pharmacist who served in an Egyptian regiment and then with the Imam of Sana'a, occupied himself amongst the inscriptions and carvings. The other two, Joseph Halévy, a Frenchman, and Edward Glaser, a German, travelled to Marib under the auspices of the *Académie des Inscriptions et Belles Lettres* in Paris in 1869/70 and the 1880s respectively. Halévy copied inscriptions and returned to Paris with nearly seven hundred. This learned work added a wealth of knowledge concerning pre-Islamic Yemen. The German, Leo Hirsch, an Arabic scholar and archaeologist, entered the country in 1893. Although he travelled in local costume, he admitted he was a European. His guides conducted him on the usual route for caravans, leaving Mukalla, on the south coast, for Wadi Hadhramaut via the ancient route of Wadi Do'an. Hirsch touched the Bavarian Baron von Wrede's route although von Wrede confined himself more to the easterly region and not to the main Wadi. Hirsch was therefore the first European to enter the main valley of Hadhramaut. Here lay the largest settlements belonging to the Qu'aiti and Kathiri states, which Hirsch visited with a guarantee for his safety from the Qu'aiti Sultan and a guide from the Kathiri tribesmen. The Qu'aiti Sultan received him well, and a poem of welcome was composed in his honour by a local bard.

Scholarly, scientific expeditions were undertaken at the end of the nineteenth century to Socotra and Abd al-Kuri: Professor Isaac Bayley Balfour's 48 days' stay on Socotra and first scientific exploration of the island was soon followed by Drs. Schweinfurth and Riebeck in 1881. They were members of the German expedition who devoted themselves largely to the study of the people and language. At the same time they collected specimens in various branches of natural history. In 1898-99, W. R. Ogilvie Grant of the British Museum and Henry O. Forbes of the Liverpool Museums made extensive researches on both islands. From these pioneering expeditions, many of the specimens found proved to be new to science, and the results were published. The scientists' achievements demonstrate the unique richness and fragility of these islands.

It has not been possible, for reasons of space, to include in this volume portraits of all those who inspired these important illustrations over the centuries – it is, in any case, their illustrations which are their memorials. An immense debt of gratitude is nevertheless owed to all of them for giving us, through their creative achievements, this invaluable knowledge of Yemen.

Right: Theodore Bent, the British explorer, accompanied by his wife Mabel, led a scientific expedition into Hadhramaut in 1893. The couple also explored other regions of South Arabia, including Socotra. *ILN*

Below: Walter Harris, British correspondent in Morocco for *The Times,* travelled to Yemen in the 1890s, during the Turkish occupation. Harris is pictured in the presence of Ahmad Feizi Pasha, Governor-General of Yemen, being questioned on the reason for his visit to Yemen. *Harris 292*

Above: Al-Hauta, the guest house of the Sultan of Lahej, where members of the conjoint British Scientific expedition stayed before carrying out their studies on the island of Socotra, in the 1890s. Unfortunately they did not stay long in the guest house because to their 'dismay we discovered that small-pox was very prevalent in the town.'   *Forbes xxii*

Right: 'After two hours' climb up the valley [on Socotra] in which was our camp, I [Dr. Schweinfurth] spent several days in a spot, distinguished by the "Teke" fig trees called "Kischen", 750 metres above the sea. Dr. Riebeck had enough camels and drivers for all our wants, but we had not sufficient tents, and so we had to betake ourselves to the natural hollows and grottoes, in our excursions ... At the beginning of May rain again began to threaten, and so I could not pass the nights under the fig trees.' *Schweinfurth 41*

GLOSSARY OF TITLES

Sayyid, Sayyida	a title denoting descent from the Prophet Mohammed through his grandson Husayn bin Ali
Sharif, Sharifa	a title denoting descent from the Prophet Mohammed through his grandson Hasan bin Ali
Sheikh, Sheikha	a title of respect; the head of a tribal group
Qadhi	a judge of religious law. Also used in Zaydi areas for any member of the hereditary class of scholars or administrators
Ulema	men learned in Muslim law and traditions
Wali	governor
Naqib	tribal chief; commander
Naib	deputy
Mutasarrif	governor (Ottoman official)
Kaimakan	Turkish officer

KEY TO AUTHOR'S ABBREVIATIONS

References under the captions have been kept to a minimum for reasons of space. For example, *Niebuhr(2)I.Pl.LXVII* signifies Carsten Niebuhr; (2) means more than one book by the same author, I is for Volume I of a multi-volume work; Pl. is Plate followed by number of the Plate in Roman figures. Often there is simply the surname of the author(s) and page number in Arabic or Roman figures i.e. *Harris 93, Forbes lxvi.*

Annesley = Annesley, George, Viscount Valentia, *Voyages and Travels to India, Ceylon, the Red Sea, Abyssinia and Egypt in the Years 1802,1803,1804,1805 and 1806,* London 1807.

Balfour = Balfour, Isaac Bayley, *Botany of Socotra,* volume XXXI of the transactions of the Royal Society of Edinburgh, 1888.

Bent (1) = Bent, Theodore, *Southern Arabia Soudan and Socotra,* London 1900
Bent (2) = Bent, Theodore, *The Sacred City of the Ethiopians being a Record of Travel and Research in Abyssinia in 1893,* London 1893.

Berg = Berg, L.W.C. van den, *Le Hadhramout et les Colonies Arabes dans l'Archipel Indien,* Batavia 1886.

Bernatz = Bernatz, John Martin, *Scenes in Ethiopia,* 2 Volumes, London 1852.

Bird = Bird, James, *Himyaritic Inscriptions, from Aden and Saba,* translated into English, *Journal of the Royal Asiatic Society,* Bombay Branch 1844.

Bizzoni = Bizzoni, Achille, *L'Eritrea nel passato e nel presente,* Milano 1897.

Bruce = Bruce, James, *Travels to Discover the Source of the Nile,* 5 Volumes, London 1790.

Carter = Carter, H. J., *A description of the Frankincense Tree of Arabia, Journal of the Royal Asiatic Society,* Bombay Branch 1847.

Dapper = Dapper, Olfert, *Naukeurige Beschryving van Asie,* Amsterdam 1680.

Deflers = Deflers, A., *Voyage au Yemen, Journal d'une Excursion botanique faite en 1887 dans les montagnes de L'Arabie Heureuse,* Paris 1889.

Elwood = Elwood, Anne Katherine, *Narrative of a journey overland from England, by the Continent of Europe, Egypt and the Red Sea, to India; including a residence there, and voyage home, in the years 1825,26,27 and 28,* London 1830.

Felner = Felner, Rodrigo José de Lima, *Collecção de Monumentos Ineditos para a Historia das conquistas dos Portuguezes, em Africa, Asia, E. America*, Lisboa 1860.

Forbes = Forbes, Henry (Ed.), *The Natural History of Sokotra and Abd el-Kuri*, London 1903.

Forskal/Niebuhr = Forskal, Peter and Niebuhr, Carsten, *Icones Rerum Naturalium, quas in itinere orientali depingi curavit Petrus Forskal, Post mortem auctoris ad Regis mandatum aeri incisas edidet Carsten Niebuhr*, Hauniae 1776.

Grandpré = Grandpré, L. de, *Voyage dans l'Inde et au Bengale faite dans les années 1789 et 1790*, 2 Volumes, Paris 1801.

Graphic = *The Graphic*, London, 1890 and 1894.

Groote = Groote, Eberhard von, *Die Pilgerfahrt des Ritters Arnold von Harff von Coln durch Italien, Syrien, Aegypten, etc. wie en sie im den Jahre 1496 bis 1499*, Cologne 1860.

Halls = Halls, John James, *The Life and Correspondence of Henry Salt Esq., FRS etc.* 2 Volumes, London 1834.

Harris = Harris, Walter B., *A Journey through the Yemen and some general remarks upon that country*, Edinburgh and London 1893.

Head = Head, Franklin Captain, *Eastern and Egyptian Scenery, Ruins &c. Illustrative of a journey from India to Europe*, London 1833.

Hemprich = Hemprich, Friedrich Wilhelm & **Ehrenberg** = Ehrenberg, Christian Gottfried, *Symbolae physicae seu Icones et Descriptiones corporum naturalium novorum aut minus cognitorum Quae ex itineribus per Libyam, Aegyptum, Nubiam, Dongolam, Syriam, Arabiam, et Habessiniam*, Berlin 1828-49.

ILN = *The Illustrated London News*, London 1867,1873,1883,1890s.

Irwin = Irwin, Eyles, *A series of Adventures in the Course of a Voyage up the Red, on the Coasts of Arabia and Egypt; and of a route through the deserts of Thebais, hitherto unknown to the European traveller, in the year 1777, in letters to a lady*, London 1780.

Looss = Looss, Arthur, *Mémoires présentés a l'Institut Egyptien*, Cairo 1896

Ludolf = Ludolf, Hiob, *Ad suam Hisotriam Aethiopicam Commentarius*, Frankfurt 1681.

Manzoni = Manzoni, Renzo, *El Yemen tre anni nell 'Arabia Felice*, Roma 1884.

Massaja = Massaja, Guglielmo, Cardinal, *I miei trentacinque anni di missione nell'alta Etiopia*, 12 Volumes, Roma/Milano 1885-95.

Molesworth = Molesworth, Lt. Gen. G.N., *Notes on a trip to Mukalla 1893*, manuscript, Royal Geographical Society, London.

Nicholson = Nicholson, B.A.R., *Notes on a shipwreck on the southern Coast of Arabia on the night of the 14th January 1836*, manuscript, Royal Geographical Society, London.

Niebuhr (1) = Niebuhr, Carsten, *Beschreibung von Arabien*, Copenhagen 1772.
Niebuhr (2) = Niebuhr, Carsten, *Reisenbeschreibung nach Arabien und andern umliegenden Landern*, Volume I Copenhagen 1774, Volume II, Copenhagen 1778.

Roque = Roque, Jean de la, *Voyage de l'Arabie Heureuse, Par l'Ocean, et le Détroit de la Mer Rouge. Fait par les Français pour la première fois, dans les années 1708, 1709 & 1710. Avec La Relation particulière d'un Voyage du Port de Moka à la Cour du Roi d'Yemen, dans la seconde Expedition des années 1711, 1712 & 1713*, Amsterdam 1716.

Rüppell = Rüppell, Wilhelm Peter Simon Eduard, *Atlas zu der Reise im Nordlichen Afrika Zoologie*, Frankfurt 1828.

Salt = Salt, Henry, *A Voyage to Abyssinia*, London 1814.

Schweinfurth = Schweinfurth, Georg, *Erinnerungen von einer Fahrt nach Socotra*, Westermann's *Illustrierte Deutsche Monatshefte*, 1891.

Shaw = Shaw, Thomas, *Travels and Observations relating to several parts of Bombay and the Levant*, Oxford 1738.

Shaw IN = Shaw, Samuel (ed.) *An Interesting Narrative of the Travels of James Bruce into Abyssinia*, London 1800, third edition.

Wellsted (1) = Wellsted, James Raymond, *Travels in Arabia*, 2 Volumes, London 1838.
Wellsted (2) = Wellsted, James Raymond, *Travels in the City of the Caliphs, along the shores of the Persian Gulf and the Mediterranean, including a voyage to the coast of Arabia and a tour of the island of Socotra*, 2 Volumes, London 1840.

ASIR

Qunfidah

R u b

N

NAJRAN

Abu Arish • *Sa'da*

Jizan

AL-JAWF

Midi

W. al-Jawf

Luhayyah

Hajjah • Marib *Ramlat al-Sa* Shabwa

Kamaran

Salif **Sana'a**

Suq al-Khamis

Manakha *Wa'alan*

Hajra *Khadar*

Hodeidah *Attura* *Wisil* *Qarat al-Negil*

Bayhan

▲ J. Doran

Bayt al-Faqih • *Dhamar* *Nisab*

W. Zabid *Yarim*

Al-Zuqur *Zabid* *Ibb* *Bayt Said*

Hays *Jiblah* *Qa'tabah* *Yafa'al-Ulya*

Hanish *Dhala* *Yafa al-Sufla*

Al-Kabir W. Bana

Ta'izz W. Khoreiba W. Tiban

Mocha W. al-Kabir *Shuqra*

Khanfar *Al-Salih*

Lahej *Shaykh Othman*

(Al-Hauta)

Perim I. **Aden**

(Mayun) *Little Aden*

Mandab GULF OF

RED SEA

R E D   S E A

T i h a m a

B a b   a l -

Inset map:

0 Km 60

Dähläk Is.

Bay of Zula

ETHIOPIA

Adulis

15°

Yeha

Adwa

Aksum

40°